SUCH IS LOVE

# SUCH IS LOVE

## *Romantic Games and Why We Play*

PETRA HASSALL

ILLUSTRATIONS BY
ANDREW HIGGINS

Matador
9 Priory Business Park,
Wistow Road, Kibworth Beauchamp,
Leicestershire. LE8 0RX
Tel: 0116 279 2299
Email: books@troubador.co.uk
Web: www.troubador.co.uk/matador
Twitter: @matadorbooks


ISBN 978 1789015 072

British Library Cataloguing in Publication Data.
A catalogue record for this book is available from the British Library.

Typeset in 12pt Proxima Nova by Troubador Publishing Ltd, Leicester, UK

Matador is an imprint of Troubador Publishing Ltd

To Sue Sutcliffe
A much valued colleague and friend
Thank you

# CONTENTS

# INTRODUCTION

*"I just don't get it, I really don't. Things were finally starting to feel better! So why did he break up now?!"*

Your friend's been slumped on the sofa for over three hours, but you're still not making any progress. All that's clear is her boyfriend's dumped her and the search is on for what went wrong.

*"Well what exactly did he say? There had to be something more than the usual rubbish. He seemed like the kind of guy who'd be straight about that sort of thing... and anyway you're right, you've both looked happier recently. It doesn't make any sense."*

*"I've already told you, the same old stuff... 'It's not you, it's me'... 'You're great, it's just not working'... 'It's not the right time for a serious relationship'. Nothing more... I swear. What am I supposed to do with any of that! Everyone knows it's meaningless."*

Her gaze shifts upwards... but as the ceiling isn't offering much inspiration she turns to you again.

*"Really, what do you think? I know we've been over it a hundred times but I'm sure we must be missing something and I definitely don't want to go through this again! If you're holding anything back... anything at all... please don't, just tell me."*

You look her straight in the eye and tell her she's amazing, she's funny, intelligent, kind and that any man would be lucky to have her as his girlfriend... and you mean it.

Ok that's true. So, what do you think is going on? After all, your friend's relationships aren't working right?

## WHAT'S THE ANSWER?

You and your friend may have already noticed her habitual attraction to the same kind of man, but how far are you prepared to go in examining her role in creating the situations she finds herself in? Why can't she form a lasting relationship if that's what she's looking for?

No matter how badly a person's behaving, and let's face it there are some real 'players' out there, if we're continually choosing relationships that cause us pain, then we're trapped in a negative pattern of behaviour as much as they are.

We're playing a 'Game'. We just aren't aware of it yet.

This book is about those Games. It isn't about the fun flirtations we play as harmless pastimes, it focuses on the compulsive perplexing and unconscious patterns that form part of the human condition and over which without awareness, we have such little control.

Aimed at all those who suspect they're playing, 'Such is Love' analyses what's going on beneath the surface whenever we're caught in a compulsive pattern of behaviour.

## ROMANTIC GAME PLAYING HAS ALWAYS BEEN WITH US. BUT WHY?

At first glance it makes no sense. Everyone wants to have human contact and we all feel a longing for love and acceptance. Instant gratification will only go so far and even the hardened lothario is often suppressing an inner world of need.

No child is born with the innate desire to deceive and manipulate others.

Games by their very nature are dishonest. Ulterior and unspoken motives run through what's happening and nothing is quite as it seems. Games stand in the way of us receiving what we long for.

# THE FIRST THING TO RECOGNISE IS THAT GAMES ARE PLAYED FROM A POSITION OF FEAR.

At the start of a new relationship, how many of these questions run through your mind?

* What would happen if I were really honest?
* How vulnerable would that make me feel?
* How do I know I haven't chosen someone who's just going to take advantage?
* Shouldn't I seek to protect myself?

The chances are you've been hurt before, your guard is up, and you could be imagining the same thing will happen again. Because you don't know why you keep finding yourself in this situation, as an act of defence you might unconsciously start to 'play'.

You've probably chosen a person who, because of their own emotional complexities, is more than able to participate. Like you, they'll also be primed to 'play', and their Game will complement yours.

It's often quite easy to see where our friends are going wrong, it's the same old story time and again; but when it comes to our own behaviour, insight can be in short supply. Yet until we understand what we're doing, how can we hope to change?

# WHEN DO GAMES BEGIN?

The Games we play begin in childhood. We observe our parent's patterns of behaviour and respond to how they relate to us. If we've found ourselves caught in situations of defensiveness, distance or pain, we often try to resolve those early life difficulties through our own adult relationships. The problem is that because we've learnt to relate through those same patterns, we're unconsciously drawn to repeat them.

We unwittingly choose a person both able and willing to play them out; then as each new relationship unfolds, our fears are reconfirmed through another cycle of disappointment.

# SO, HOW CAN THIS BOOK HELP?

This book clearly shows these patterns, so you can start to address them.

It contains a total of eight Games, each devoted to a relationship pattern. The characters are fictional, but their dilemmas are based on my clinical observations over many years as a psychotherapist. Except for Game 3 all the Games are played by two people.

* Each chapter begins with both parties giving an honest account of how they're feeling and why they believe they're behaving this way.
* There is then an analysis of the unconscious drivers behind their actions.
* This is followed by a section devoted to what they can do to change.
* Finally, we are told what happened next.

Whilst a huge number of variables go into creating who we are as individuals, we all share certain psychological drivers. These drivers are outlined and interlinked throughout the Games.

If you don't directly find your own dynamic in one of these Games, you will nevertheless see the building blocks that have helped to create your familiar pattern of relating.

Ultimately this book offers choice. Choice to decide if you wish to stop, or whether you prefer to keep on playing.

# COME ON IN

## THE TALE OF JACK AND POLLY

# JACK'S TALE

*"The place was crowded I remember that... but mostly I remember her. You know how it is when you meet someone: a snapshot moment, flash! and they're there!*

*Her hair was scrunched back in a ponytail, with a fringe coming down to her eyes. Blue eyes... really piercing. They were smudged round the rims with mascara and kohl.*

*'Wow!' I thought. 'She's beautiful'.*

*The boots were black, and her body was wrapped in a little grey dress... the picture of a girl who would never be short of attention and I can tell you one thing, she certainly had mine.*

*'Hi,' she smiled, 'can I share your table?'*

*'Sure, no problem.'*

*My paper seemed suddenly much less interesting and just as I was wondering how to get her attention, she spoke.*

*Polly was single, and life was fun. She loved guys but didn't want anything serious.*

*'Great!' I said and meant it. What luck!*

*Initially the date was going to be drinks but it turned into so much more! Polly seized everything. It wasn't just sex, though that was amazing... it was what we got into afterwards. She opened me up and I told her stuff... about myself, my feelings, that I never* tell anyone. Polly did the same, I swear, and although looking back I can see it sounds stupid, I really thought she was the One... that I'd met my soul mate. I was sure.

The next few weeks were pretty intense. We saw each other constantly and all I wanted was to be with Polly. If she was busy, we'd endlessly text, our messages fuelled by jokes and sexy banter. I just couldn't get enough of her.

Then one day about six weeks in... she ghosted me!

I couldn't quite believe it at first, I kept thinking there must be some mistake. After she didn't respond to my texts or calls I went round to her place, but no one was in. I know it's pathetic; I even started imagining something had happened to her; but as we didn't have any friends in common and she never seemed to bother with Facebook, who could I contact or call? God, it felt desperate.

Then a few days later I bumped into this girl who I'd seen her with once at a bar. The awkward silence said it all... it was clear I'd just been dumped. Her friend couldn't get away fast enough and I was left feeling like a complete idiot.

Guys don't talk about girls who ditch them. The most you'll get is some stupid comment or an 'I wouldn't bother if I were you, mate'. And, ok, she was a 'player'; I've met them before... in fact, I seem to be a bit of a sucker for them. You know the ones: they make it amazing then drop you from a very great height. Men do it all the time, right? So, who am I to complain? But what happened this time? It felt so real. And yeah, sure, there was the no-strings statement, but why get in so deep? I hate that... the whole 'I told you no strings as they prise out your heart.

But I can tell you one thing: I'm not going to let it happen again."

# POLLY'S TALE

*"Oh, you mean that guy, yeah I know, he probably thinks I'm a complete cow, right? Men often think that... even though I tell them from the outset I'm not looking for anything serious.*

*We met in a crowded cafe one morning. The tables were taken and when I saw him there lost in his paper, there was definitely something... a cuteness, I guess... hard to put one's finger on it. I just knew I wanted his attention.*

*The following Friday as we perched on our bar stools he looked really sexy, so we went back to his. I was right it was great, but later as we lay together feeling relaxed I found myself telling him stuff I don't usually bother getting into. He did the same... but he just wouldn't stop! By the time I left it felt like we'd gone too far. I couldn't wait to get home.*

*He texted the following day... Jack, his name was... and to be honest I wasn't sure what to do. In the end, I guess I just thought 'Why not?' There's something empowering about knowing a guy's keen, I feel more attractive, more vital, somehow, and striding down the street with a spring in my step I can see men turn to look.*

*I called him and turned up the charm. I don't even know why I bothered, it wasn't as if I had to. Anyway, he landed up at mine and we had a great time.*

*The next few weeks were so intense, and I found myself getting in deep in a way I'm not comfortable with.*

*It's happened before, a guy piques my interest and before I know it I'm being swept along on a tide of excitement and emotional intensity; but it always ends up feeling the same... like I'm being suffocated. It's enough to drive you crazy.*

*What else can I say? Well, he texted me constantly... even when I told him I was rushed off my feet... always expecting an immediate response. God, it was needy! And if there's one thing I just can't stand, it's having to deal with those kind of feelings... it's way too much.*

*So, I ended it. I just didn't return his calls. Yes, I know, but what could I say? Your neediness is suffocating me? I couldn't say that! It would have ended up being one of those 'it's not you, it's me' conversations and what's the point? Better just to walk away. Ok, maybe I'm a coward, I don't know, but life can get so complicated it feels easier just to leave.*

*I've got this friend, Julie, who's always on the other end of this kind of thing. I'm hugely sympathetic; I know what a lovely girl she is and that any guy would be lucky to have her in his life, but I've told her a million times, 'Stop going for commitment-phobes.' Which I guess is what I am too.*

*The irony is of course that a couple of times when I've been keen, the guy goes off and dumps me! Men certainly seem to have more of a reputation in that department, but to be honest it cuts both ways.*

*God knows. The whole thing makes no sense, but I'm young and free and I know which end I'd rather be on. The one who's in control."*

# WHAT'S THE GAME?

'Come On In' is a very common Game. It can be played at any point during a relationship but is at its simplest when encountered in the first few weeks.

'Come On In' is a Game that centres on the distortion of power and the interrelationship between the roles of 'victim' and 'persecutor.'

It can be distinguished from the normal process of getting to know someone or the genuinely casual fling, by the fact that emotional insecurity and the need to control dominate the action.

The more positive qualities of curiosity, empathy and pleasure are present in Jack and Polly's encounter, but because they're subservient to the demands of the Game they're unable to alter the underlying dynamic.

'Come On In' begins when each party unconsciously assigns themselves a role, one as 'victim', the other as 'persecutor', then the action builds until someone decides to stop playing. They do this by either directly confronting what's happening or more commonly by simply withdrawing from the Game.

In this scenario it's Polly who chooses the role of 'persecutor', whilst Jack becomes the 'victim'. Neither is consciously aware of what they're doing, and both would be horrified to think of their actions in such stark terms.

Jack and Polly aren't 'players' in the conventional sense of the word; life is more complex than that. Their involvement, however, has less to do with an honest engagement than with both parties' unwitting ability to play their part in the Game of the other.

## POLLY

When Polly meets Jack there's something about him that immediately awakens her interest. It isn't simply her desire to be noticed and admired by a man but something subtler in Jack's presence that tells her she's found a participant. This is the unconscious draw.

Polly: *"there was definitely something... a cuteness, I guess... hard to put one's finger on it. I just knew I wanted his attention."*

We're all primed to instinctively choose a person willing to participate in the pattern of behaviour we're caught in, and Polly unconsciously recognises a participant in Jack.

When she says she isn't looking for anything serious she means it, but Polly's motivations are complex. Her willingness to go deeper suggests she's looking for greater emotional intimacy than she's consciously aware of.

Polly: *"I found myself telling him stuff I don't usually bother getting into."*

However, intimacy evokes a sense of vulnerability in Polly that is profoundly uncomfortable. It has the capacity to awaken her own feelings of need, buried beneath a superficial confidence.

Polly: *"The next few weeks were so intense, and I found myself getting in deep in a way I'm not comfortable with."*

So, what is it about Jack that Polly unconsciously picks up on?

Because Polly is both drawn to emotional intimacy yet fearful of feeling need, what attracts her to Jack is an unconscious awareness that she has found a man capable of playing the needy one in the relationship.

Polly: *"he texted me constantly... even when I told him I was rushed off my feet... always expecting an immediate response. God, it was needy!"*

To understand this further we need to look at two interconnected psychological phenomena that Polly and Jack are experiencing: projection and projective identification.

# PROJECTION

A comprehensive analysis of projection appears in Game 5, 'Will You Be My Movie Star?', but here is the definition:

DEFINITION

Projection is the psychological mechanism by which we attribute to other people our own unconscious impulses and personality traits. Projection doesn't refer to those half-acknowledged characteristics we attempt to disown in ourselves but are quick to observe in others; it occurs when we have absolutely no awareness the quality in question belongs to us.

In this scenario Polly is projecting her neediness onto Jack.

Polly doesn't realise that the needy feelings she's rejecting in Jack belong as much to her as to him. She has so successfully shielded her conscious mind from the strength of her own need she's blind to the fact that she's criticising Jack for the very emotion she's denying in herself.

Jack *is* intrinsically needy, but the reason why Polly is repulsed by his need is because at some point in her life she was rejected for being needy. Polly possesses unconscious feelings of shame around her own neediness and this renders the emotion unbearable to her.

# PROJECTIVE IDENTIFICATION

There's more however than straightforward projection going on between Polly and Jack.

Polly is also pushing her needy feelings directly into Jack through the unconscious act of projective identification.

> ### DEFINITION
> Projective identification is a complex psychological state, but at its heart it's essentially a game of 'emotional pass the parcel', where undesired and difficult feelings generally existing outside the realm of conscious awareness are passed from one person to the other without either being aware of what's happening. When it occurs, a person can actively start to experience an emotion belonging to another.

Polly: *"if there's one thing I just can't stand, it's having to deal with those kind of feelings."*

Jack is getting a double whammy. Not only is he having to contend with his own feelings of need; he's unconsciously acting out Polly's neediness as well.

Jack: *"The next few weeks were pretty intense. We saw each other constantly and all I wanted was be with Polly. If she was busy we'd endlessly text [...] I just couldn't get enough of her."*

Often in intimate relationships, but sometimes in more casual encounters, we find ourselves experiencing feelings which essentially belong to the other person: this is projective identification.

Whilst Polly might have some understanding of her own emotional complexities, it's insufficient for her to be aware of what's going on, and Jack certainly doesn't know.

So, whilst Polly ultimately rejects Jack, she stays in the relationship for as long as she does because she can unconsciously cast off her own need.

Polly: *"I feel more attractive, more vital, somehow, and striding down the street with a spring in my step I can see men turn to look."*

Polly's aware that having a guy who's *"keen"* is empowering, but she isn't conscious that this essentially false sense of empowerment comes at the expense of another.

When Polly disappears without explanation, she justifies it by claiming that all she could offer Jack would be a meaningless break-up trope. Emotional honesty is ruled out as being too hurtful, but how she chooses to act is far more persecutory.

Polly's scared of what Jack's response might be. Part of her is fearful that if confronted Jack might prove unwilling to simply play the role of needy 'victim'. Neither does she want to be openly cornered into the role of 'persecutor', even if he's willing to go along with it. It's safer to simply walk away.

Polly states that whenever she's been keen the guy has dumped her and this suggests two things:

Her neediness is much closer to the surface than is superficially apparent.

Polly is firmly caught on the emotional axis where one person is the 'victim' and the other the 'persecutor'.

Whilst we persecute people for a variety of reasons, the roles are always essentially interchangeable. We do not persecute unless on some level we are fearful of becoming the 'victim' ourselves.

# JACK

Is Jack right to feel victimised by Polly?

In one sense, yes. Polly has led Jack on by saying one thing, doing another, then dumping him.

She claims she isn't looking for anything serious then immediately invites emotional intimacy before playing her 'get out of jail free card' of 'I said no strings' when confronted with powerful feelings.

But Jack is participating in this.

His belief that an easy encounter can turn into something serious is plausible if taken slowly, but by becoming so quickly involved with someone who says that's not what they're looking for, Jack is setting himself up for disappointment and rejection.

However unlikely it seems, this is exactly what Jack is unconsciously looking for. Towards the end of the narrative he tells us that similar situations have happened in the past.

Jack: *"And, ok, she was a 'player'; I've met them before... in fact I seem to be a bit of a sucker for them. You know the ones: they make it amazing then drop you from a very great height."*

This suggests Jack is repeatedly drawn to women whose behaviour promises emotional fulfilment but who dump him once he gets involved.

Both Jack and Polly are experiencing repetition compulsion.

DEFINITION

Repetition compulsion is the unconscious desire to compulsively repeat a painful relationship pattern and/or early life trauma. The longing is always for a different outcome, but because the compulsive behaviour creates the same emotional dynamic, instead of resolution the original experience is simply repeated.

On some level both Jack and Polly must have felt their emotional needs were unacceptable whilst growing up, so experienced the neediier part of themselves as rejected and unloved. They are just responding differently to the same painful experience.

On a conscious level Jack is attracted to Polly's no-strings statement because it implies he won't get hurt, but unconsciously he's repeatedly striving for resolution and acceptance, whilst choosing women who will reject him again. This has the effect of reinforcing his belief that women will invite him in then walk away.

Polly states that she has become involved in situations of emotional suffocation before, and this highlights her own repetitive behavioural pattern:

Polly: *"It always ends up feeling the same... like I'm being suffocated."*

So, what happens if someone repeatedly finds themselves in the role of 'victim'?

People caught in the role of the 'victim' often feel powerless and mistreated. Unfortunately, their strategy for change can sometimes be to become the 'persecutor', which ultimately serves them no better.

If we take a pessimistic view of Jack's romantic prospects, then we would have to conclude that one of two things will happen: either Jack will continue in the role of 'victim' and repeat the pattern, or he will decide that all women are heartless, so he's going to persecute them, as they have him.

Jack: *"But I can tell you one thing: I'm not going to let it happen again."*

There is however an alternative.

# POSITIVE STEPS FOR CHANGE

Both Jack and Polly need to examine their early childhood relationships to help identify the compulsions they're currently wrestling with. But they must also examine their relationship to power.

Power is an essential component in the roles of both 'victim' and 'persecutor', and the defining characteristic of 'Come On In'. The role of 'persecutor' is the obviously powerful one, but the role of 'victim' is not without power itself.

Polly as the 'persecutor' gains the immediate high of feeling the power that comes from rejecting her own neediness and ostensibly being in control, but Jack as the 'victim' occupies the moral high ground. An object of pity and compassion in the eyes of others, a 'victim' may be perceived by some at least as all heart.

'Victims' can use pity to manipulate others, thereby gaining power and control in a subtler, but equally distorted fashion.

This position works better for women than men, as gender stereotyping ensures that men are often perceived as weak, if superficially powerless. As such, they're less likely to stay in the role for long and generally prefer to be the obvious aggressor.

The realisation needs to come from both Jack and Polly that regardless of the position they adopt, power is present. Whilst trapped in the realm of Game playing however, it will only exist in distortion and never bring lasting happiness.

# JACK

The moment Jack realises that as the 'victim' he possesses as much power as Polly and is equally responsible, he will feel liberated. The Game will unravel before his eyes and he will have choice.

Recognition of one's role is the first step to change.

At the end of the narrative Jack states he's had enough, but his comments suggest he's in danger of simply switching positions.

Jack: *"But I can tell you one thing: I'm not going to let it happen again."*

If, alternatively, he can see his part in the problem, then when it comes to a new relationship, rather than judging himself or the other person, he will approach what's happening in a spirit of curiosity and look at what he's helping to create.

# POLLY

Polly seeks emotional intimacy but is in denial of her own need. She too will have experienced rejection in early childhood but has learnt to cope by adopting the opposite position to Jack.

The problem is, the role of 'persecutor' is ultimately no more satisfying, for it can only be maintained through emotional isolation.

Polly's position is harder to shift, as she appears happier with the immediate pay off.

Only at the point when she's truly had enough and her desire for an intimate relationship is stronger than her need for self-protection and control will there be any possibility for change.

# EPILOGUE

## JACK

*"I saw her again quite out of the blue, at the cafe where we'd first met.*

*It was oddly timed, as I'd just started seeing this new girl, Ella. Things were going ok, I guess, but far from the rollercoaster ride I'd experienced with Polly and my eyes were immediately drawn to her.*

*Ella's sweet, unassuming, but a bit too needy... there sat Polly, wearing the same grey dress.*

*She was chatting to some poor sod, completely oblivious to my presence... and as I looked at her smiling, batting her eyelashes, for a moment an uncomfortable mixture of anger and desire rose up inside me. Then my girlfriend came to mind... her eager face, hopeful, kind... and I was overcome with pity... for me, for her... I don't know... it's hard to explain.*

*I got up, went home and just sat there thinking, 'what do I actually want?'*

*I've no idea where I'm going with this, but I do know one thing: I'm not just dumping that girl like Polly dumped me. I'm going to try and work it through.*

*And maybe the relationship won't be long-term, who knows,*

*but I need to tell Ella how I'm feeling and where I've been in the past. Then ask her what's really going on for her.*

*It takes two, after all."*

# POLLY

*"I saw him out of the corner of my eye and pretended not to notice.*

*How awkward!*

*The guy at the table was smiling, engaged, he appeared to be totally into me; but the conversation suddenly seemed stale. I made my excuses and left.*

*Later that evening I called Julie.*

*'Am I a cow in the way I treat men?'*

*'No of course not! You go after what you want and get it! Better that than being like me, good for you.'*

*But somehow it seemed like we'd missed the point and I didn't even know what that was. I felt a bit lost, uncertain... feelings I really dislike.*

*I don't see my parents much and to be honest my mum isn't that interested, but I picked up the phone and called my aunt. I'm going to see her next weekend... I just need to talk things through."*

# SUCH A SWEETY

## THE TALE OF LUCY AND JOE

# LUCY'S TALE

*"I used to have this friend called Dan. He lived next door and we'd play after school... Dan, me and his sister Megan. Whenever I was with him I'd have great fun, and as Dan wouldn't do girl's stuff I'd often find myself climbing trees or playing computer games. Megan wasn't interested in that sort of thing.*

*My parents were busy a lot of the time, so Dan's mum would let me stay for tea. I didn't kid myself; I knew in my heart that Megan came first, but Dan had this way of making me feel like his second sister... so even though sometimes I felt on the fringes that was good enough for me.*

*I've never been one to get too close. My own mum liked her space and it was clear that Dad would get on her nerves with his constant questioning and need for attention. No brothers or sisters, one was enough. I was an independent child.*

*Anyway, Dan met Sarah. It was a few years ago now and at first it seemed ok. Then last June they had the big white wedding and ever since then he's dropped away.*

*They say it happens when people get married – perhaps she saw me as a threat; who knows – but she isn't interested in being friends and although I'm invited to the odd group thing I can feel myself being edged out. It's a bit upsetting when I think about it and in a weird kind of way reminds me of when we were children; I would see him watching television through the window with his sister... they were just happy together without me. Megan often wanted him to herself.*

*Then about four months ago Joe stepped into my life. We met at a bonfire party quite by chance... which for more than one reason I shan't forget. It was fine at first, well at least the fireworks were great; but as the evening wore on things had seriously started to get out of hand. Some idiot had almost fallen in the fire and everyone was obviously drunk. So, after advising Jessica that she really ought to put the fire out! I'd moved inside to escape the madness. And that's when I saw him... Joe Ferragosto, the picture of the self-assured man. He was tall, laid-back and lounging on the sofa. What else could I do but suggest I join him.*

*We flopped down together and started to chat. Joe was relaxed and good humoured, so when he commented on the evening's events I found myself laughing them off. I didn't want to seem uptight... Lucy the go-getting tomboy is always a better idea. Joe was obviously entertained, and his own conversation was so full of stories and fun, that by the end of the evening I didn't think twice about giving him my number.*

*At first it was great. Joe knows everyone; he's lively and popular with a list of friends as long as your arm. He didn't seem to mind that I need my space... why should he? he's constantly busy... and, to be honest, at first I really made an effort to get involved. I like to put my best foot forward at the start of a relationship; guys always seem to want a girl who's willing to jump right in. Besides, it was just so great to be around him that no real effort was required.*

*For the past few weeks, however, I've become increasingly aware that his texts are getting more constant. They're always very loving but a bit too much and the other day when I told him I was having a girls' night out he was decidedly off with me.*

*There even seemed to be a suggestion I wasn't quite telling the truth. When I pointed this out he apologised and said of course it wasn't a problem, but I didn't like his unwarranted suspicion and It's starting to feel as if everything revolves around him.*

*Occasionally he'll do some guy thing... girls not required... and I find myself fitting my own friends round his requirements.*

*So, I've started to go 'off radar' sometimes, even if he's trying to get hold of me, and this is clearly a problem. But you can't be around someone all the time... I thought he understood.*

*A few years ago, I dated this guy who became hugely resentful that he wasn't the centre of my world. Dan would make jokes about it, calling him the 'limpet' and in the end I dumped him. It was just too much.*

*Dan isn't around now, of course. I felt like calling him the other day... then didn't. It's his life and I guess he's moved on.*

*I look at Joe and see the kind of guy I've always wanted. He's handsome, popular, successful and kind, but I just crave a bit more space. I'd be mad to end it though, I do really like him. I'm not sure what to do."*

# JOE'S TALE

*"Yes that's right, she's called Lucy Winterbourne... ironic really as her birthday's in June. Although I'm starting to notice there's a coolness of manner which may yet prove her name quite apt.*

*When I first set eyes on her my instant impression was of somebody slightly apart; but, God, she looked lovely and the attraction that sparked was just too strong to ignore.*

*It was last November on Guy Fawkes Night, the 5th had been a Saturday so Jess put on a show; fireworks, a bonfire and barbecued sausages... everyone seemed to be itching for fun. But when Jack Cassidy almost fell in the fire I decided to go inside. Even I can have too much of a good thing.*

*I crashed on the sofa, whiskey in hand, when at that moment Lucy strolled past.*

*'Hi, do you mind if I join you?'*

*'You're welcome.'*

*As she sat down beside me I couldn't help smiling, she looked so attractive and sounded so warm, I assumed my impression when I'd seen her outside must have simply been wrong.*

*'Had enough of the chaos?'*

*Lucy laughed.*

'Perhaps... although I do like my fair share of mucking about; I used to be a champion tree climber in my youth.'

I must have looked surprised because she laughed again... reaching over as she did, in search of the whiskey. I poured her a glass and before I knew it three hours had flashed past. Lucy just seemed happy and so engaged, of course, I asked for her number.

I've known a few girls in my life I guess, and it's easy enough to make friends... but Lucy's special. She's always fun to be around... lively and intelligent... someone who knows how to get stuck in.

Most of the time things are great between us, we enjoy the same things and Lucy's got a cracking sense of humour... not to mention a really sexy laugh. But then for no reason she just goes silent and fails to answer my calls. It seems to come out of nowhere and always manages to throw me.

At first, I pretended I wasn't that bothered, but now it's starting to make me annoyingly suspicious. I can see she tries to fit her life round mine and I appreciate it, but why does she just stop responding to my texts or suddenly cancel last-minute? When I ask her, she says she didn't hear her phone, or felt tired and out of sorts. Then she'll be really loving, and it feels like I'm making a fuss about nothing, which I probably am.

This sort of thing has happened before... girls who appeared so keen then started mucking me about. Even my mum used to do it. When I'd come home from school in the afternoon, I was never quite sure what I'd find. It wasn't her fault... life was just a bit difficult.

Lucy seemed different, though, not like the relationships I've had in the past and certainly not like my mum. So, I've started to wonder why my romantic life always seems to go awry. It's not like I think all women are unreliable. I don't; I have some great female friends who are totally there for me. I wish I fancied one of them!

*Maybe I just expect too much from a girlfriend. I never have a problem with friends. But a girlfriend should be different, right? The relationship closer.*

*It would just be nice to feel like I really knew Lucy; she's wonderful in so many ways and I want to make it work."*

# WHAT'S THE GAME?

'Such a Sweety' is a game of greater subtlety than 'Come On In'.

'Come On In' is structurally simple. The central theme is 'victim' and 'persecutor', with the key component power.

'Such a Sweety' has a different emphasis. Its focus lies on the attachment style we develop in childhood, and the impact this has on our relationships in adult life.

Lucy and Joe *do* wrestle with the issues examined in 'Come On In'. Distortion of power is a common theme and can be found, if looked for, in 'Such a Sweety'. The difference is it doesn't define the action in the same way.

All eight Games described in this book possess overlapping themes. Each can range from mildly annoying to highly destructive and the degree to which the players are damaged is dependent on the intensity and commitment with which the Game is played.

## INITIAL ATTRACTION

Why do Lucy and Joe come together?

When we first meet someone our attraction will centre on what we consciously desire: Is he intelligent, witty, loyal, hardworking...? There will be hints at the outset of the deeper draw, but the extent to which we notice can often be inhibited by three things:

1. The mask of social grace initially worn.
2. The desire often present, to be more accommodating than is realistically sustainable.
3. The willingness to ignore what we may have glimpsed, but have swiftly put out of our minds.

Close friends are likely to see what's happening, when the same old pattern starts to unfold, but the actual participants remain blind for much longer or are capable with effort of crushing their doubts.

When caught in a repeated relationship pattern it's worth noting that, however different a person superficially appears, our own unconscious compulsions are probably blinding us to what we would otherwise realise: this one isn't different.

The initial impression Lucy and Joe have of each other demonstrates two potential pitfalls with first impressions:

1. Because Joe's socially confident, Lucy's perception of him is significantly at odds with how he relates in close personal relationships.

Lucy: *"And that's when I saw him... Joe Ferragosto, the picture of the self-assured man."*

2. Joe *does* pick up on Lucy's need for distance, but her subsequent behaviour helps him discount what he'd consciously rather not notice.

Joe: *"When I first set eyes on her my instant impression was of somebody slightly apart."*

Joe: *"she looked so attractive and sounded so warm, I assumed my impression when I'd seen her outside must have simply been wrong."*

Like Jack and Polly in 'Come On In', Lucy and Joe are caught in repetition compulsion.

---

### DEFINITION

Repetition compulsion is the unconscious desire to compulsively repeat a painful relationship pattern and/or early life trauma. The longing is always for a different outcome, but because the compulsive behaviour creates the same emotional dynamic, instead of resolution the original experience is simply repeated.

---

This is a common motif of all games. By their very nature they are repetitive patterns of behaviour circling continuously back to the beginning and creating increasing frustration.

# JOE

Joe makes a choice at the start of the relationship to see Lucy as the girl *"who knows how to get stuck in"*. This, after all, is that aspect of her character he consciously desires.

Joe's unconscious attraction, however, stems as much from Lucy's need to distance herself as it does from her willingness to engage. It's Lucy's need to pull away that is the compulsive component in Joe's attraction.

In being unable to cope with Joe's emotional needs Lucy is helping facilitate the repetitive cycle of disappointment Joe is caught in, one where his most intimate relationships prove unpredictable and feel unsafe.

Joe: *"This sort of thing has happened before... girls who appeared so keen then started mucking me about. Even my mum used to do it."*

Joe is completely unaware of his own unconscious compulsion to repeat this pattern; in fact, Lucy's withdrawal is exactly what he consciously fears.

Lucy unwittingly assists in Joe's blindness. Not only does she want to spend more time with Joe at the start of their relationship; she's also initially willing to be more accommodating than is comfortable.

From childhood Lucy's learnt to alter her behaviour to gain attention:

Lucy: *"as Dan wouldn't do girl's stuff I'd often find myself climbing trees or playing computer games."*

Lucy: *"to be honest, at first I really made an effort to get involved."*

Joe meanwhile masks the extent of his emotional need.

Joe: *"At first, I pretended I wasn't that bothered, but now it's starting to make me annoyingly suspicious."*

By compromising their own needs to too great an extent both Lucy and Joe create the impression they're happy to give what the other wants when the reality is very different.

# LUCY

From Lucy's perspective Joe gives the impression of someone unlikely to cling. Joe is the *"picture of the self-assured man"*, popular and at ease.

Lucy has experienced emotional distance in childhood, so struggles with intimacy in adult life.

Lucy: *"I've never been one to get too close. My own mum liked her space."*

Unlike Joe, she requires a very slow pace of development to cope, but Joe is unable to tolerate this. Any withdrawal on Lucy's part will immediately generate suspicion and clinginess in Joe and this in turn will cause Lucy to feel overwhelmed, provoking a need to distance herself further.

Lucy: *"So, I've started to go 'off radar' sometimes, even if he's trying to get hold of me, and this is definitely a problem. But one can't be around someone all the time..."*

Because Lucy's and Joe's initial impressions of each other are at odds with what lies beneath, neither is consciously aware of what they're getting into.

*"... I thought he understood."*

To understand how Lucy and Joe have developed such different styles of relating, we need to look at attachment theory.

# ATTACHMENT THEORY

### DEFINITION

Attachment theory is a theoretical model that takes as its focus the relationship formed between a child and their primary caregiver. The attachment style we develop as children is a key contributor to how we relate in adult life.

If a child experiences a consistently loving and caring relationship, particularly in their first few years of life, then feelings of safety and trust will develop, which translate into an ability to create secure adult relationships.

If, however, a secure attachment fails to be established and no other significant figures such as grandparents or teachers surface to help mitigate the problem, relational difficulties will start to develop, which continue into adult life.

This manifests most clearly with romantic partners, who often carry an enormous weight of expectation in terms of emotional fulfilment. A person who can relate well or certainly adequately with colleagues and friends may still face difficulties when it comes to romance.

It's clear from Joe's narrative he has the capacity to choose reliable female friends, but when it comes to greater intimacy the combination of his own unconscious choice of partner and the level of attention he needs and demands from close relationships starts to prove overwhelming.

Whilst attachment theory has a complex and nuanced structure, for the purposes of this book I will focus on the three most common attachment styles: *secure, ambivalent* and *avoidant*.

*Secure attachment* arises when the child has developed a safe, straightforward and loving relationship with their carer. They trust they won't be abandoned and believe in their caregiver's capacity to contain their emotional needs.

*Anxious ambivalence*, by contrast, occurs when an individual has been exposed to an unpredictable level of responsiveness. The primary caregiver will sometimes have been loving and receptive but too often insensitive and unavailable. Such behaviour generates a sense of uncertainty and confusion in the child, which is then carried forward into adult life.

The *anxious avoidant* has had a more straightforward experience. Through reliance on a caregiver who has been regularly unresponsive to their emotional needs, they grow either consciously or unconsciously to expect rejection. As a result, emotional intimacy feels unsafe.

# JOE

Joe's attachment style is *anxious ambivalent*. The way he vacillates between distrust and dependency is exactly in keeping with the response an infant has when experiencing emotional unpredictability, and suggests he's acting out an early childhood pattern.

As an adult the anxious ambivalent is often self-critical and insecure one moment, then demanding and possessive the next. This helps explain why Joe feels anger and resentment when Lucy doesn't provide the reassurance he needs but is reluctant to express his feelings out of fear of rejection.

In his narrative Joe is careful not to consciously blame his mother for her own unpredictability.

Joe: *"It wasn't her fault... life was just a bit difficult."*

He is likewise reluctant to blame Lucy.

Joe: *"it feels like I'm making a fuss over nothing, which I probably am."*

By relying too heavily on others to validate their self-worth, the anxious ambivalent often provokes the very outcome they fear: their partner leaves them. This is in danger of happening to Joe.

## LUCY

As an *avoidant,* Lucy is wrestling with a very different problem. Her early life experiences have left her with a profound reluctance to express need. This suggests that her mother's desire for *"space"* was experienced by Lucy as rejecting. The avoidant child learns that by not crying or being overly dependent they can at least remain in physical proximity to the caregiver. Lucy is probably carrying either the conscious or unconscious belief that any expression of vulnerability will result in rejection.

The childhood relationship she formed with Dan and Megan mirrored that sense of emotional isolation.

Lucy: *"I would see him watching television through the window with his sister... they were just happy together without me."*

If we look at Lucy's relationship not only with Joe but also Dan, we can see that in different ways each result in emotional distance.

Joe overwhelms. His need for Lucy to build her life entirely around him is disproportionately possessive and Lucy pulls away.

Dan is unavailable; there's always another woman between him and Lucy. It's therefore safe to indulge in fantasies of intimacy with Dan precisely because they will never be realised. In secretly longing for an unavailable man Lucy precludes the possibility of a meaningful relationship with someone who's present.

Both these relationships feel unsatisfying because they fail to answer Lucy's basic human need: to be known and cared for intimately.

# REPEATING THE PARENTAL PATTERN

Lucy's choice of Joe is also driven by another unconscious motivator. Their relationship appears to mirror that of her parents.

Lucy: *"my own mum liked her space and it was clear that Dad would get on her nerves with his constant questioning and need for attention."*

In choosing Joe, Lucy is unconsciously repeating the relationship pattern she witnessed as a child.

Joe doesn't mention his upbringing in any detail, but it would be unsurprising if he was doing the same.

We often choose partners whose pattern of relating allows us to repeat what we know. Even if we experienced our parent's relationship as dysfunctional, its familiarity exerts an unconscious and sometimes irresistible pull.

Once we recognise this pattern, however, we gain choice, and with it the power to alter our behaviour.

# POSITIVE STEPS FOR CHANGE

In an ideal world both Lucy and Joe would have chosen someone with a secure attachment style, who could contain their anxieties more easily. Their relationship, however, still holds possibility.

Lucy and Joe both possess qualities genuinely attractive to the other and aren't simply ruled by compulsion. If viewed in a positive light their coming together creates the potential for laying an intergenerational pattern to rest through choosing to relate differently.

This is not to underestimate the difficulties. Familiarity has the power to draw us forward, but change creates uncertainty and fear. Lucy and Joe need to demonstrate not only awareness but also empathy for the problems each separately face.

# LUCY

Lucy must examine her feelings for Dan if she wishes the relationship with Joe to flourish.

As mentioned earlier, she may unconsciously be using her residual feelings for Dan as a vehicle for intimacy avoidance and Dan, at least prior to the wedding, appeared complicit in this. His comments on her previous boyfriend resembling a *"limpet"* suggests two things:

Joe is not the first person Lucy has experienced this with.

Dan in the past was not above encouraging Lucy's feelings by denigrating her boyfriends.

Lucy is fortunate she's being *"edged out"*. If she can finally let go of Dan, this will give her the opportunity to focus her feelings on a relationship with Joe.

# JOE

Joe needs to become more aware of how focused he is on his own emotional needs. Because he's always thinking of Lucy he's under the erroneous impression this is the same as really considering what *her* needs might be.

Joe's emotionally very young. In many ways he's still the anxious and insecure little boy longing for mummy's love. As such, Joe's unconsciously relating from a highly ego-centric position. If he can bring a more adult awareness to what's happening, he can start to monitor and contain his emotional reactions before feelings of insecurity overwhelm him. This will offer breathing space for Lucy.

# TOGETHER

Above all, Lucy and Joe need to have an honest conversation about how they're feeling. Joe is not the only needy one in the relationship: Lucy's avoidance is masking a reservoir of need, dammed up inside her. Both must be prepared to make allowances for the difficulties the other is facing.

If Lucy and Joe are willing to take on the challenge, they can start to find strategies to help them cope with problems as they arise.

Joe certainly appears ready for this. He's starting to question why things are consistently going wrong in his romantic life and this is always the first step towards change.

Romantic relationships by their very nature encourage inflated expectations of what our lover is capable of. If we've experienced difficulties in childhood there's often an unconscious expectation that our beloved will magically right all the wrongs of our past. This is accompanied by a corresponding unwillingness to recognise them as a flawed human being.

Even though Lucy and Joe's relationship has started in fantasy, it can continue through acknowledgement of the truth.

By focusing on the positive qualities of the other, assuming responsibility for their own compulsions and being empathic to the problems each separately face, the path to acceptance and change will open, affording Lucy and Joe the opportunity to make their relationship work.

# EPILOGUE

## LUCY

"I bumped into Megan last Friday. We hadn't spoken in ages, so when she asked why I'd missed Dan's party I was taken completely by surprise. I said I'd been busy, but it wasn't true, I hadn't even known it was happening! They kept that quiet.

After we parted I went back home... seething inside at his ghastly wife. Why did she want to push me out? What had I ever done to her?

I lay on the sofa feeling miserable when a text appeared from Joe... aaaargh! Why couldn't he just leave me alone?! I picked up the phone and threw it across the room... watching with sudden desperation as it skidded towards the wall. Thwack!

After frantically scrabbling for the scattered pieces I burst into tears! I must have cried all afternoon... it certainly felt that way. Dan had only ever been a friend. Couldn't Sarah see that?

After a while I just lay there motionless, staring blankly at the ceiling. I had a lovely guy and a great life... what was the matter with me?

When I'd calmed down I texted Joe and asked if he was still

*free. We're meeting for supper at mine but I'm not sure what to do. Something feels close to snapping inside."*

# JOE

*"As usual Lucy didn't respond for hours! Then finally she called and asked me to supper... and as usual I said yes!*

*When I arrived, she was cooking a Bolognese. The table wasn't laid, and she looked quite tired; I think she might have been crying. The atmosphere felt fragile somehow and her hair was pushed over her face.*

*I got out the cutlery and uncorked the wine, when suddenly she burst into tears!*

*'This isn't like you, Luce; what's wrong?' I put my arms round her and we just stood there for about five minutes; saying nothing.*

*Then it all came out. How hard it was, how much she cared about me and wanted to make it work... if only I could give her more time and just let it breathe... perhaps we could get there.*

*So, I said how I was feeling. Everything. My stupid suspicions, my fears... but most of all, how much I cared for her too.*

*We're going to try... both of us. I'm sick of going around in circles and there's so much here that's great. There has to be a way forward."*

# THROUGH THE LOOKING GLASS

## LOOKING GLASS

### THE TALE OF ISOBEL, SUZIE AND BOB

# ISOBEL'S TALE

*"Belle and Bob... yes, really.*

*My father keeps calling us Bill and Ben... even though I've repeatedly asked him not to. And there's no changing it. I've asked B more than once, 'How about Robbie or even Rob?' but he won't... he just carries on using the same old name, regardless of how I feel about it.*

*We've been living together for quite a while and things are going well. No fireworks, it's true, but what do you expect from a steady relationship? Besides, B works in compliance, so I wasn't imagining a thrill-seeker. Someone I can rely on: that's what I'm looking for.*

*We've even started talking about buying a house. I'm tired of renting; it just feels so impermanent. My parents have promised to help with the deposit and anyway it's time to settle down. I don't want to be one of those people whose continually shifting from one place to another; there's a lot to be said for security. Bob seems ok with the idea but nothing's finalised. He can be a bit closed when it comes to anything serious; he'll either sit on the sofa not saying a word or crack some stupid joke! No conflict; he's steady and reliable... well... he always used to be. There've been a few things recently, which if I'm honest I'm not that sure about.*

*Odd little incidents have started happening; nothing in themselves, but they're beginning to add up. The other day his phone rang whilst he was in the shower and when I answered the person just hung up. The name came up as Steve, someone I've never heard of, but when I asked B who it was, he just said a work colleague. Why would he have a colleague's number in his phone who he hasn't even mentioned in passing? And why would they be calling at the weekend?*

*He's also been doing a lot of overtime recently and a couple of weeks ago he went on a guys' weekend away arranged at the last minute. Nothing was said about what happened or who was there, which definitely isn't like Bob, and when I questioned him more closely he got quite cross.*

*I'm not naturally suspicious and I don't like telling people what to do, but yesterday evening when he was late again I decided to log into his emails and see what I could find. When I tried to get in, however, his password had changed and the password on his laptop had been altered as well. I don't know what to do... I can't exactly challenge him; it would look like I was snooping, but whenever I ask why he's staying out late he just says he's got a lot on. A lot of what?*

*It's all a bit unsettling because this isn't Bob's normal behaviour. He's knows I like to know where I stand.*

*It's the big 3-0 next year... as friends keep reminding me, and I feel like I've invested a lot in this relationship. We saw this sweet little house last Saturday and my parents agreed to go with us next week to have another look.*

*I've always thought Bob would make a reliable husband and that's what I want. Nothing extraordinary; just a well-ordered life.*

*Maybe I shouldn't be telling you this, but things weren't always easy when I was a child... not the perfect family my friends imagined. There wasn't any shouting as such, but Mum just seemed so tense and Dad would often stay out late or be off on one of his business trips. I don't know; my sister never seemed that bothered and I didn't like to ask or make a fuss; who knows what they'd have said.*

*Anyway, I guess my parents want to do something nice and property is so expensive these days, this is our chance.*

*So, if Bob's just going along with it surely things have to be ok... right? Why else would he want to buy a house?"*

# BOB'S TALE

*"Hi, yes, I'm Bob. Ok... where to begin?*

*I'm with this girl, Belle. We've been seeing each other for about three years, living together for one, and she's making it massively clear she wants to settle down.*

*I like her; don't get me wrong. Belle's always been organised and besides it's easy, never having to think about shopping or sorting out drinks down the pub with friends... not to mention holidays, Belle's queen of the last-minute deals. But, Christ, she's bossy... over every little thing. She even keeps nagging me to change my own name... just because of some stupid joke her dad keeps making! You wouldn't catch him changing anything.*

*Up until now it hasn't really bothered me; if I don't want to do something I just ignore her. That always worked with Mum and it works with Belle too. I learnt early on in life it's easier to seem like you're towing the line... and if you want to have a laugh son, then do it behind the bike sheds or the fun police will be down on you like a ton of bricks! Who wants to go looking for trouble? My relationship with Belle might be dull but at least I know where I stand.*

*The problem is there's this new girl in the office and it's more than just a casual flirt, I can't seem to get her out of my mind. In fact, we've already started seeing each other.*

*Suzie's so free! No plans, no nagging, no commitment. Just fun. If anything, I'm telling her what to do! I organised this weekend away in Brighton... making up some story to Belle... and Suzie acted like I was trying to pin her down! But she came, and it was amazing! She dragged me off to the nudist beach and ran into the waves, shouting and waving. I felt so alive!*

*The other day, though, she called at the weekend and Belle picked up the phone. Luckily, I had her down as a bloke – I'm not completely stupid – but B was definitely suspicious. I didn't say anything to Suzie; I didn't want it to turn into one of those 'it's over' conversations... I'm just having such a good time... but I've changed all my passwords so Belle can't pry, and I'm going to have to say something to Suzie... I'm just not sure how to put it.*

*Belle's talking about buying this house with a deposit her parents are giving us. I'm thirty-four and perhaps it's time to start settling down. I don't know, Suzie's great but you can't live like that... it just doesn't feel very stable. Belle's got to be the way forward, but, God, it's boring. I feel like I'm forty already and the pressure to get me to propose will be next.*

*If I carry on with Suzie everything could blow up in my face. I'm not sure I can trust her to keep it secret. I just don't know what to do."*

# SUZIE'S TALE

*"Yes, I know what you're going to say.*

*'Why are you getting involved with a guy who's already with someone?' But I've never been one for commitments and at first it just seemed like a bit of fun.*

*I'd joined this company and was struggling to find my feet. Bob was so helpful; he knows everything about compliance and is really patient. Even if I pull a face or start to act stupid when I don't understand, he doesn't seem to mind; he just cracks a joke then carefully explains again.*

*Being with Bob has started to feel like being held in a safe pair of hands... something unusual for me. I've had a few flings that were meant to be fun... and even a couple of long-term relationships; but it doesn't seem to matter if it's a guy or a girl: everyone turns out the same... selfish and unreliable. So, yes, I know he's got a girlfriend, but he's never hidden it from me... it's not like he's trying to lie.*

*At first, we didn't even discuss the whole girlfriend thing... keep it light, that's my style. I'm so used to people who're ready to leave, I just pretend I couldn't care less. But things are shifting and not because of anything I've said. A few weeks ago, quite out of the blue, he started talking about Her. Saying how bossy she is and how dull his life has become.*

'Well what are you going to do to spice it up?' I said, so he went off and booked a weekend in Brighton!

At first, I was like, what's going on here, is he serious?! But we had such a great time I'm starting to have real feelings for him.

I find myself thinking about him constantly and the other day I called his mobile at the weekend even though I knew I shouldn't... I guess I just wanted to see what would happen. His girlfriend answered and I hung up immediately, but I wasn't sorry... part of me is starting to want her to find out.

Bob said nothing on Monday morning and neither did I, but surely if he was that committed to this Belle girl he'd have ended it there and then? I just need to give it more time... maybe he'll be the one to offer some security."

# WHAT'S THE GAME?

'Through the Looking Glass' picks up on a theme previously discussed in 'Such a Sweety': the issue of emotional honesty.

The situation that Isobel, Suzie and Bob find themselves in is the logical outcome of more than straightforward deceit. It stems from all three participants' emotional evasiveness as much as it does from Bob's ready willingness to lie.

The irony is that everyone involved expresses a longing for emotional security, but the individual belief systems governing their actions are creating a self-destructive cycle of behaviour likely to result in the reverse.

So, what are the belief systems creating this scenario?

*Isobel* has been brought up in a don't ask questions atmosphere, where underlying tension is ignored in the hope that by saying nothing the problem will go away.

*Bob* has learnt that to be 'acceptable' he must conform to certain patterns of behaviour and bury the more fun-loving aspects of himself. This has led to frustration and deceit.

*Suzie* has experienced past relationships as unreliable and rejecting, so is struggling with the belief she's unworthy of love. She therefore plays the 'I don't care' game, whilst secretly longing to feel secure and loved.

Isobel, Suzie and Bob are all lacking a strong sense of internal emotional security.

As outlined in 'Such a Sweety', internal emotional security is an important factor in enabling us to create secure external relationships. A secure sense of self creates a willingness to be vulnerable, as there is less fear of having one's weaknesses and perceived inadequacies 'exposed'. All three participants are reluctant to fully express themselves out of fear of rejection.

# ISOBEL

Isobel suspects Bob is having an affair but feels unable to confront him.

Whilst she may outwardly appear bossy, Isobel's equivocal response to Bob's behaviour suggests an underlying insecurity hidden behind a need to control.

In her narrative she describes unexplained undercurrents within her family that troubled her but which she felt unable to openly address.

Isobel: *"There wasn't any shouting as such, but Mum just seemed so tense and Dad would often stay out late or be off on one of his business trips."*

Isobel has avoided facing her fears of what may have been happening in her parents' marriage. The atmosphere of suppressed tension experienced in childhood, however, has unconsciously informed her adult choice of partner.

Like Lucy in 'Such a Sweety', Isobel is in danger of repeating her parents' relationship pattern by effectively taking a cue from her mother's behaviour, the key message being that preservation of the marital relationship is worth the cost of tension and discontent.

This message has become a *script*.

---

### DEFINITION

Scripts are thought patterns learnt in childhood that through constant repetition come to dictate how we see ourselves, our place in society and the nature of the world we live in.

---

*Scripts* can either be positive or negative in nature.

Negative examples: I am ugly; the world is against me; men are unfaithful; you can't trust.

Positive examples: I am intelligent; most people are fundamentally kind; if I work hard I can succeed.

Whether others agree with our scripts is irrelevant, if we believe them, they hold enormous power and can effectively become self-fulfilling prophecies.

The earlier a script is ingrained, the tighter we cling to it. We grow to see these thought patterns as being part of who we are and relinquishing them feels like relinquishing a part of ourselves. Many people go through life with damaging and erroneous beliefs about themselves because of what was repeatedly conveyed to them as children.

## FAMILY DYNAMICS

This doesn't mean that everyone in Isobel's family received the same message as Isobel. Scripts can work collectively to create a sense of family identity: 'We the Johnson's are this...' but they also exist individually or in complementary pairs: 'I'm the good girl; my sister is naughty.'

Isobel states that her own sister "*never seemed that bothered*" about the unspoken undercurrents in her parent's marriage, and it's worth noting that several variables are always at play when it comes to the experience of an individual child within any family grouping:

1. The child's inherent personality traits.
2. How that personality informs their relationship with other members of the group (e.g. 'Daddy's girl'; 'your sister reminds me of...'; 'you're just like your father!').
3. Their birth placement: eldest, middle, youngest, only.
4. Their gender, and the parental expectations attached to this.
5. The personality the group creates collectively: the 'we'.

Individual children can experience what is ostensibly the same upbringing very differently. It's therefore risky to generalise from one child to the next about the impact their family has had upon them.

Isobel's experience will have been unique.

# BOB

Bob understands Isobel's need for safety (even if his understanding is not entirely conscious) and he has conflated this with the belief that the spontaneous aspects of his own personality must be split off to maintain their relationship.

We don't have sufficient information to know if this is true, but Isobel certainly seeks to be in control, implying spontaneity may appear threatening.

Why is Bob willing to split off a part of himself to be with Isobel?

Isobel has become a 'mother figure' for Bob.

Bob has unconsciously chosen a woman who shares similar characteristics to his real mother.

Bob: *"That always worked with Mum and it works with Belle too."*

He's acting out a familiar pattern of behaviour and like Isobel is probably replicating the dynamic between his parents:

Bob: *"I learnt early on in life it's easier to seem like you're towing the line... and if you want to have a laugh son, then do it behind the bike sheds or the fun police will be down on you like a ton of bricks!"*

Bob wants Isobel to take care of him.

Bob: *"Belle's always been organised and besides it's easy, never having to think about shopping or sorting out drinks down the pub with friends."*

For this to happen, however, he believes he must be a 'good boy', with the wilder, 'unacceptable' aspects of his nature kept out of sight, as in childhood.

His relationship with Isobel as it stands is preventing Bob from fully expressing himself, so he's playing with Suzie to gain fun and freedom.

Bob appears to have little awareness he's actively betraying Isobel's trust and, whilst Suzie's phone call would have indicated her own growing emotional involvement, he's choosing to view her no-commitments statement as a green light to use her.

Bob: *"I didn't say anything to Suzie; I didn't want it to turn into one of those 'it's over' conversations... I'm just having such a good time."*

Bob is unconsciously choosing to jeopardise his relationship with Isobel by having an affair with Suzie, a woman who has the kind of unpredictable energy likely to lead to discovery. This implies that Bob is uncomfortable with his need to split off an aspect of himself.

He may unconsciously want 'mother' to fully accept him for who he is, so is seeking to be found out. In any event, Bob appears willing to risk an end to the relationship rather than continue to feel stifled, but his feelings are confused.

# SUZIE

Suzie, like Isobel, is refusing to see what stands in plain sight.

She explicitly states she's often been involved with unreliable and selfish lovers but seems unaware that Bob's behaviour is also deceitful and selfish. Suzie sees Bob as reliable and safe.

Suzie: *"Being with Bob has started to feel like being held in a safe pair of hands."*

This flies in the face of the obvious truth that Bob is deceiving Isobel and reflects how deep-seated Suzie's own patterns are.

Repeatedly getting into relationships with people who operate from a position of dishonesty and ultimately reject her implies a belief in Suzie that she's unworthy of love and therefore deserving of abandonment.

We are told nothing of her childhood or family circumstances, but Suzie's fun-loving persona suggests that, contrary to Bob, she's likely to have received attention and praise for being spontaneous and free. Any expression of emotional need, however, may have been frowned upon, as this is an aspect of Suzie's personality she seems anxious to suppress.

Suzie: *"At first, we didn't even discuss the whole girlfriend thing... keep it light, that's my style."*

Consciously Suzie sees Bob as *"different"*. Her attraction is based on his capable, almost fatherly attitude: the *"safe pair of hands"* she longs for. But unconsciously she's attracted to someone, where any stated desire for emotional security will result in abandonment. Suzie has no internal sense of emotional security and this is being mirrored in her external relationships.

Ironically, it's this very lack of security that prevents Bob from seeing her as more than fun.

Bob: *"Suzie's great but you can't live like that... it just doesn't feel very stable."*

Bob himself is not as secure as Suzie imagines. He too longs to be the little boy in the safe pair of hands, able to play freely with 'mummy' in the room. So, although Isobel is insecure and controlling, her behaviour is quite literally more familiar to Bob. Suzie is therefore likely to face rejection, even though she offers much that Bob craves.

# POSITIVE STEPS FOR CHANGE

If there's to be any hope of shifting these behavioural patterns, Isobel, Suzie and Bob must all be willing to confront their motivations and fears.

# BOB

Bob needs to make a clear decision about whether he wants to stay with Isobel. At present, he's unconsciously abdicating responsibility onto Suzie to make that decision for him.

If he decides he does want to stay, what next?

The first problem is that Bob is already having an affair. With a much longer and more established relationship there is an argument for the transgressor to remain silent.

Confession can often be embarked upon in the conscious belief one wishes to be honest, but in reality it's being used as a mechanism to alleviate feelings of guilt, largely achieved at the expense of burdening the other.

Unless there's a desire to confront what's led to the instigation of the affair and a willingness to address this, confession itself can form part of an elaborate Game played out in a complex and difficult marriage.

This is not the case, however, with Isobel and Bob, whose relationship is of a comparatively brief duration.

If Bob confesses, it will act as a catalyst for him and Isobel to examine what's going on between them, but any chance of their staying together will depend on Bob's willingness to accept responsibility for his actions. Attempting to evade responsibility with 'you made me do it' will prevent the possibility of repair.

It will then be for Isobel to decide not only if she's willing to continue their relationship in what will inevitably be an atmosphere of broken trust but also whether she feels able to fundamentally address the way they relate.

# ISOBEL

Whilst Isobel may have unconsciously chosen Bob to repeat her childhood experiences she's not consciously aware of this. In his confession, as in his affair, Bob will be leading the action. Isobel may not be ready to explore her own underlying feelings.

What are Isobel's options?

1.  Isobel can end it with Bob, placing the blame firmly at his door and in time enter a relationship with someone else. This runs the risk the same thing will happen again, just with a new participant.

2.  She can forgive Bob and decide to stay in the relationship. However, if the underlying problems are not addressed the likelihood of further infidelity is strong. Bob will still be living in an atmosphere where he feels unable to fully express himself, so is likely to become a serial offender. Things may fail to reach a head for many years and then at much greater cost to all.

3.  Isobel can decide the affair has caused an irreparable breach and end the relationship. Unlike option 1, however, she's willing to look at the dynamic created with Bob and start to address where her fears and insecurities lie.

4.  The final option is that Isobel tells Bob she's willing to try, but they must both be honest about their expectations and needs within the relationship.

This will require Isobel to be far more transparent about her own emotional insecurities and the relevance these have on her need to control.

Such a conversation is going to be difficult. Although Bob is already aware of Isobel's need for safety, any open acknowledgement of how insecure she feels will challenge Bob's view of Isobel as the person who's there to offer *him* security.

Bob has grown used to attributing to Isobel an essentially parental role, and an honest discussion, where Isobel is no longer 'bossy mother', could shift the way they relate into unfamiliar and initially uncomfortable territory.

The parent/child dynamic is currently the hallmark of Isobel and Bob's relationship, and the fact things clearly aren't working doesn't make a shift any less unpredictable or scary.

Such a challenging situation may require an outside impartial mediator such as a couple's counsellor, to help them work through what's happening. We should not underestimate the power of unconscious drivers and both Isobel and Bob will have to be determined to create change.

# WHAT ABOUT SUZIE?

Even if Isobel and Bob split up, it's unlikely the relationship between Bob and Suzie will work.

They might stay together for a while, but the chances are they will then separate.

Suzie is not going to be able to meet Bob's need for a stable 'mother'; she's looking for a parental figure herself. As Bob has chosen Suzie for fun-loving freedom he's unlikely to be able or willing to meet her emotional needs either. Bob is just too insecure at present to hold Suzie safely.

In the worst-case scenario Bob will abdicate all responsibility for what's happened and blame Suzie for the breakdown in his relationship with Isobel. Suzie will be labelled 'the other woman', coming between 'the happy couple' by leading Bob astray.

Suzie needs help.

Currently Suzie appears to unconsciously believe that any expression of emotional need will be met with rejection, and, whilst she copes by expressing an attitude of no commitment, her feelings for Bob demonstrate the corrosive quality of constructing such an easily pierced defence mechanism.

Suzie is the victim of Bob's casual willingness to use women, but because she's chosen a man already involved with someone else her role as the 'victim' is obscured by Isobel's more obvious claim.

Unlike 'Come On In', where Jack and Polly fall into an easily identifiable external pattern of 'victim' and 'persecutor', Suzie's 'victim'/'persecutor' axis demonstrates more clearly the internal nature of the problem.

Suzie is choosing inappropriate lovers to unconsciously persecute herself. She does this because on a profound level she has learnt to be ashamed of her own vulnerability and need.

She was never really looking for a casual fling; she just doesn't believe she's worthy of a proper commitment.

'Through the Looking Glass' is a tale of the longing for safety and acceptance, in the face of insecurity and self-doubt.

That vulnerable aspect of Suzie that is struggling to find a haven needs to be fully acknowledged and accepted by Suzie herself. If she can achieve this she'll be more able to show herself the care, compassion and love she so desperately needs. Suzie's search for external love can then be conducted in a more grounded and honest fashion.

# EPILOGUE

## ISOBEL

*"Well it all came out. Last Saturday.*

*'Steve' got in touch again... but this time there was no mistaking what was going on.*

*We were in the park enjoying a picnic with friends and Bob had just finished a phone call from his mum. He threw down his jacket and went to play football when I heard the familiar tweet. I just had to pick it up.*

*'Hi sexy can't wait 'til Monday at mine xxxx'*

*I just sat there staring, not sure what to do. Jenny looked over my shoulder and her face said it all... I knew she'd read it. Now everyone was going to find out, Jennifer Graham can never keep her mouth shut.*

*'I already knew,' I said. 'I was just deciding what to do.'*

*She didn't say anything, nothing at all. I felt completely humiliated.*

*I'm not sure how I got through the rest of the afternoon but, somehow, I did. When we got home, Bob went for a shower and I looked at his phone. The text had gone. For a moment I wasn't sure if I'd imagined it, but the memory of Jen's face reminded me.*

*There was the most terrible row! At first, he actually had the nerve to deny it! But when he realised I wasn't the only one who knew, he immediately changed his tack. Suddenly everything was my fault! How bossy I was, how boring life had become! I started screaming at him uncontrollably. How dare he blame me!!! He left for his parents' that evening and I just felt blank. I'd known, of course.*

*That was almost a week ago now. He texted on Wednesday and I've agreed to see him tomorrow, but I don't know what to do.*

*I told my sister... I wouldn't normally, but I had to speak to someone and I certainly didn't want the pity of a friend.*

*She just shrugged!*

*'Bob's always seemed like a bit of a 'player', she said 'He reminds me of Dad.'*

*So I was right about Dad! Why didn't she say anything? Why didn't I? I knew she knew! I wanted to get into the whole Dad thing right there and then, but she had to go to work... so I didn't. To be honest she wasn't very sympathetic, but Lil's never had a serious boyfriend so how can she understand how I'm feeling? So alone."*

# BOB

*"Belle found out. I guess she was going to if it carried on.*

*It happened last Saturday and all because I forgot to switch off my stupid phone! What the hell was Suzie thinking texting me at the weekend! I should have ended it after her previous phone call.*

*I tried to deny it... I'd seen the text and deleted it immediately. But when Belle told me Jennifer Graham had seen it too, I knew there was no point. Christ!*

*So, what did I do? I completely lost it and told her just how boring she'd become! It felt so unfair... why was I getting all the blame, when basically it was Belle's fault! I would never have behaved like that if she wasn't such a tiresome control freak.*

*Big mistake! I thought she'd never stop screaming, and in the end I just had to leave.*

*I sat in my bedroom at my parents' home feeling like crap and wondering what to do. Then I marched into work on Monday morning and ended it with Suzie. I just can't be involved with someone that untrustworthy.*

*I've texted Belle and we're meeting tomorrow. I've decided to beg her to have me back. How could I have been such an idiot, I really need her.*

*I haven't told my parents; I just said we'd had a row, but with motormouth Jenny in the mix you can be sure all our friends know.*

*I guess I'm going to have to see what Belle says. Why do I act like this?! It always ends up getting me into trouble if I try and have a bit of fun... I just never seem to learn!"*

## SUZIE

*"He dumped me... just like that. It was horrible.*

*He genuinely had the nerve to say I couldn't be trusted! But when I come to think about it, he's the one who's been having the affair! Not me!!*

*I confided in Kate from accounts and she told me he'd tried it on with Jade Simpson six months ago. Jade just has more sense. Kate was sympathetic, but I could tell she thinks I've been stupid. Apparently, everyone knows; they just haven't said anything. I haven't been at the company long, but you'd think someone would've warned me what an untrustworthy flirt he is.*

*I'm thinking of leaving, I feel so humiliated!*

*My real friends have been lovely. I know what they're thinking, though. 'Here we go again.' Vyla's been hinting as much for weeks and when I told her it was over she just sat there and asked me why I was constantly getting involved with people who muck me about. But it just seems to happen. In fact, it's they who're attracted to me!*

*I really need to sort this out... speak to someone... do something. It was obvious to everyone else that he's a total creep and I'm sick of feeling rubbish about myself. My friends are always telling me how great I am; I just wish I could believe them."*

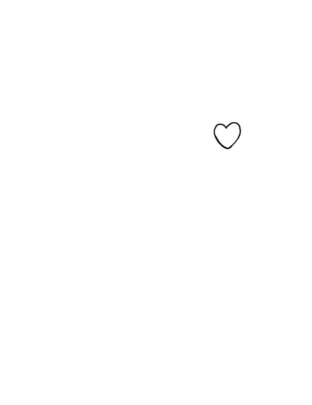

# NOUGHTS AND CROSSES

## THE TALE OF ROHAN AND PRIYA

# ROHAN'S TALE

*"It's happened again! Yes, again! And I'm getting pretty sick of it.*

*It'd been Greg's birthday... you know, that annoying guy in accounts who always picks his teeth. So, we'd all agreed to head down the pub, nothing special that's for sure; but as soon as I walked through the door she started!*

*'Why are you always so late! Don't you have any consideration for my feelings?! I've been slaving away for hours over a special meal for you!'*

*... (a) massive exaggeration! and (b) did I ask you to?!...*

*'And you just stroll in late as usual, having totally failed to text me once, or even reply when I texted you! Well I'm sick of it! You can take this relationship and stuff it! I'm leaving!'*

*Why is it EVERY time I put a foot wrong according to the book of Priya it's always the same reaction: nuclear! I have to talk her down on a bi-weekly basis; saying I didn't mean it, saying how sorry I am and that things will be different next time, saying how much I love her. But the fact of the matter is I've never done anything wrong! It's her! And, by the way, if I didn't look at my phone so what! Why should I? And why should I have to text her with an hourly update of my movements. I've been coming home early all week, has she been grateful for that?!*

*But what did I find myself doing? You're not going to believe this: I started saying sorry! Again!*

*I sat there trying to look contrite, telling her how special she was and how much I loved her. Then, when I sensed the atmosphere was changing, I asked what I could do to make it up! She burst into tears... she always does this... and said I had no idea how my just disappearing made her feel. I hadn't disappeared; I'd gone down the pub!*

*Experience has taught me however that pointing this out is entirely the wrong way to go, so I reached out and held her until she started to slowly calm down. We ended up wrapped in each other's arms with me saying how much I loved her again, only this time with more feeling, and her purring contentedly whilst we watched another romantic comedy!*

*I think I need to say at this point that I do love this girl. She's sweet and kind and beautiful. After eighteen months together, I still really fancy her and when she's not being a total basket case we have a great time. But this endless need to know what I'm doing every second of the day is starting to drive me crazy and sooner or later if it keeps on happening, I'm going to tell her to leave."*

# PRIYA'S TALE

*"Why is Rohan always doing this to me?! In many ways we have a wonderful relationship. He knows how to make me laugh and we love the same things. In fact, when we're together I can't imagine being with anyone else. But he seems to think he can live his life without acknowledging we're now officially a couple. When you move in with someone everybody knows that things have got to change.*

*Last Thursday is a prime example. I'd been working hard for what felt like days on some endless blog for a friend, so I knocked off early, poured some wine and decided to cook a great meal.*

*Rohan had actually started coming home on time, so it didn't even occur to me that if he was going to be late he wouldn't even bother to text! I thought we'd finally sorted that one out. After hours of marinating, chopping and searing, the meal was finally ready... but Rohan was nowhere to be seen.*

*I texted him repeatedly, trying to find out where he was... no response! Instead he strolled in two hours late full of booze and bonhomie, but without a single word of apology! I just went ballistic and found myself threatening to leave. Even then he didn't offer an explanation, beyond some lame story about Greg in accounts who I know he thinks is an idiot. He just kept saying how special I was and how much he loved me.*

*Well if I'm so special why doesn't he even bother to pick up the phone?!*

*In the end I relented. Rohan has this way of getting around me by looking like a little boy lost. I know... it's pathetic, but I'm ashamed to say it works every time. I found myself bursting into tears; he wrapped his arms around me and before I knew it I'd melted.*

*We curled up on the sofa to watch a movie and for the rest of the evening everything was lovely.*

*So, the question is: why can't he just be a bit more considerate, instead of repeatedly exasperating me? It's exhausting and unnecessary when all I want is a happy relationship."*

# WHAT'S THE GAME?

In the previous chapter, 'Through the Looking Glass', we focused on the issues operating beneath the surface of a relationship. Whilst it would be possible to revisit these themes, particularly in relation to attachment theory, instead we're going to concentrate on the here and now of Rohan and Priya's argument, using the method of Transactional Analysis.

Transactional Analysis is a useful tool if you suspect an argument is brewing.

## TRANSACTIONAL ANALYSIS

Transactional Analysis is a psychotherapeutic model originally devised by Eric Berne, the Canadian psychiatrist who formally identified interpersonal Game playing in his book 'Games People Play'.

It is broad in scope and multifaceted in structure, but this chapter will focus on one core aspect: the step-by-step analysis of any conversation, verbal or non-verbal, occurring between two or more people.

TA posits the theory that our minds are divided into three separate 'ego states' – Parent Adult Child – and in any interaction we are either consciously or unconsciously relating to each other from one of these three 'states'. During a conversation we often shift from one 'state' to another and when this occurs the other person consciously or unconsciously notices and alters their own position accordingly.

# PARENT, ADULT, CHILD

The terms Parent, Adult and Child do not have the same meaning as in everyday language; they are more complex, fluid and nuanced than any literal reading would imply. There are however similarities.

* The *Parent* is the deep-rooted voice of authority planted by figures of our childhood.
* The *Adult* is that aspect of ourselves able to consider and evaluate what is happening in the present.
* The *Child* represents our feeling selves, often dominant when we are experiencing strong emotion.

(NB. In 'Through the Looking Glass' whilst Isobel and Bob's relationship pattern places Isobel in the role of Bob's 'mother', their unconscious re-enactment of the parental relationship is far deeper than the fluid and shifting conversational patterns outlined in TA. The Parent/Child dynamic as defined by transactional analysis would be noticeable in Isobel and Bob's verbal and non-verbal transactions, but as a parallel process.)

We are going to focus on Rohan and Priya's argument by tracking the 'ego states' as they shift between them.

# ROHAN AND PRIYA

During their encounter neither Rohan or Priya communicates from the Adult position. Instead, they shift between the various subdivisions of Parent and Child. These subdivisions largely reflect the responses an actual parent and child have towards each other: nurturing, critical, controlling, compliant, rebellious.

Initially, Rohan and Priya's transactions are what is termed 'crossed' or discordant in nature, but as the conversation progresses their transactions shift and become increasingly 'complementary', enabling at least temporary harmony to be restored.

Let's track the conversation.

As soon as Rohan walks through the door, Priya adopts the 'ego state' of Critical Parent:

Priya: *"Why are you always so late! Don't you have any consideration for my feelings?!"*

She then appears to shift from Critical to Controlling Parent, seeking to exert power over Rohan by threatening to leave.

Beneath the surface, however, Priya is responding from the position of Demanding Child, reacting out of fear of abandonment.

To try and defuse the situation, Rohan responds as Compliant Child, submitting to Priya's anger until she begins to relent. But Rohan's acquiescence is purely superficial; he's not Compliant but Rebellious.

Rohan: *"What did I find myself doing? You're not going to believe this: I started saying sorry! Again!"*

Rohan is angry. His 'complementary' position is insincere, and his actual position is 'crossed'.

Throughout the first half of the conversation Priya's apparent 'ego state' is that of Parent, whilst Rohan responds from the position of Child.

As the conversation progresses, however, Priya openly shifts to the position of Child, the underlying 'ego state' she's been holding all along. In doing so, she alters the dynamic.

The shift occurs when Priya bursts into tears and Rohan puts his arms around her. Priya now openly adopts the 'ego state' of Submissive Child.

Priya: *"I found myself bursting into tears; he wrapped his arms around me and before I knew it I'd melted."*

In direct response to Priya's shift, Rohan becomes Nurturing Parent.

Rohan: *"I reached out and held her until she started to slowly calm down."*

By moving from anger to distress, Priya comes closer to expressing her underlying feelings of abandonment. Warmth of feeling grows between them and transforms their interaction into something genuinely 'complementary'.

Rohan: *"We ended up wrapped in each other's arms."*

Rohan is now in the position of Parent and Priya Child.

## WHAT CAN WE TAKE FROM THIS?

Regardless of how one might view relationships that have a habit of operating from the positions of Parent and Child, rather than Adult to Adult, if it's acceptable to both parties it's up to them.

The problem, however, with Rohan and Priya's use of the Parent – Child axis, at least within the context of this argument, is that it enables both to avoid addressing the more serious issue now familiar to this book: that of emotional honesty.

The nearest they come to an honest engagement, is when Priya moves from Parent to Child, adopting an 'ego state' more closely allied to her true feelings. But Priya is still caught in self-deceit: By cooking a special meal for Rohan without letting him know, particularly when it's clear that Rohan's failure to update her on his movements is already a bone of contention, Priya is setting them up for another argument.

Rohan avoids addressing his own frustration at all. He knows his unannounced lateness will cause a problem but refuses to acknowledge any prior awareness that Priya will be upset. This makes it clear that at least part of Rohan is trying to make a point. He certainly gets more than he bargained for.

Fundamental dissatisfaction with the way the relationship is working lies at the heart of the problem and provokes each to create an argument. Neither, however, seems able to openly discuss their underlying concerns, preferring expectations to remain unspoken.

Priya: *"When you move in with someone everybody knows that things have got to change."*

The fundamental and more serious argument will happen eventually, as both Rohan and Priya possess an unconscious desire to bring tensions to the surface. This temporary deferral is not helpful.

# POSITIVE STEPS FOR CHANGE

Rohan and Priya need to address their difficulties from the Adult position.

Unlike the Parent and Child, our Adult ego state exists without internal divisions, so can clearly evaluate a situation and respond accordingly.

This requires that both parties participate.

If either Rohan or Priya chooses to ignore the other's Adult attempt to address the problem, but instead responds from a position of blame, the issue will remain unresolved and the situation will become even more frustrating.

Why would anyone choose to block the opportunity for clarity of understanding?

When we clearly state our expectations, feelings, desires and disappointments, there's often the fear that a compromise won't be found, and our relationship will end. It takes courage to be honest.

By conducting the conversation through the medium of Parent

and Child it's easier for Rohan and Priya to kick the emotional can down the road, deferring the possibility of discovering irreconcilable differences.

Judging by Rohan's closing remarks, however, it hasn't been kicked very far.

Rohan: *"sooner or later if it keeps on happening,* I'm *going to tell* her *to leave."*

It may prove possible for Rohan and Priya to successfully address their problems if they start talking Adult to Adult. Their relationship will certainly collapse if they don't.

# EPILOGUE

## ROHAN

*"It came to a head last Sunday, after weeks of aggravation... and all because of football!*

*I often have a kick about at the weekend, then a pint down the pub with mates. It's pretty informal... just a bunch of friends and a place to let off steam.*

*When Priya moved in I stopped going so often, but it's important to make the effort, at least once in a while... particularly if someone asks you to.*

*Anyway, Carlo called last-minute and practically begged me down the phone to join them. A few of the regulars weren't going to make it and he was trying to pull together a team.*

*'Sure,' I said. 'No problem. Just give me half an hour and I'll meet you down there.'*

*I started rifling through the bedroom drawers in search of my kit... then Priya walked in.*

*When I told her my plans, you'd think I was confessing a crime! The usual angry upset because I hadn't 'consulted' her first. Aaargh!*

*Only this time I wasn't having it. I could see exactly where the* conversation was heading... shouting followed by tears... followed by me staying to console her and missing the fun!

'Look,' I said 'We really need to talk, but not right now. Right now, I'm going to meet the guys and get in a well-deserved game.'

'Well, if you do, then don't be so certain I'll be here when you get back!'

'Up to you,' I said, and left.

I didn't talk about it down the pub; the mood was high and who wants to hear about my personal problems... I'm sick of them myself. When I got back she was sitting on the sofa... eyes red and swollen... and I knew I had to say something. Only she started first.

'I think we need to talk about what's happening between us, because we don't seem to have the same expectations around how this relationship should work.'

'Look, Priya, I love you, we have a great time together and I love being with you, but right now I'm just not ready to give up my freedom in the way you seem to want. I'm sorry if that isn't right for you and I'm really sorry if I gave you the wrong impression, but you need to decide what you want to do, because I know it'll be a while before I'm ready to settle down and these endless arguments just aren't working.'

She left the following morning and it was really rubbish. What I most regret is how we just slid into something without having a proper conversation about what we both expected.

We haven't completely split up. I do really like her and in the long term it could work, but I don't know where it's going right now. I guess time will tell."

# PRIYA

*"I've moved out... and although I'm unpacked and sitting in my sister's spare room I still can't believe it's happened.*

*Trust it to be football to prove the final straw. Rohan did the same old thing he always does... just one phone call and he was ready to head out the door. It didn't even occur to him to ask what I wanted... of course not... and even though he could see I was really upset he still left.*

*I sat there feeling miserable, mulling over all the things he'd done... then eventually rang Nadia. She didn't mince her words; she just said we had to have a proper conversation about what was going on between us. I thought about it and knew she was right, so when he walked through the door, hours later, I grabbed the bull by the horns and said exactly what I was thinking... no drama.*

*I'd imagined he'd say how sorry he was, but instead he responded in a really straight way. I was left in no doubt: he just wasn't ready to settle down... and, although he didn't explicitly ask me to leave, what else could I do? It just wasn't what I thought I'd signed up for when we decided to live together.*

*We're still seeing each other... sort of... but whilst I'm willing to carry on like this for a while I'm not going to hang on forever. Who knows when Rohan will be ready to make a proper commitment... I want a home and a family and a man who wants that too.*

*I guess we should have both been a bit clearer from the outset, and I'm aware that part of me was scared if I stated my expectations he'd run a mile... but then he shouldn't have asked me to move in, right? I don't know... you certainly live and learn... and in the meantime, we'll just have to see how it goes."*

# WILL YOU BE MY MOVIE STAR?

## THE TALE OF STANZY AND SAM

# STANZY'S TALE

*"My parents called me Constancy. I know you're right: too much, it's true, but try telling that to my mother. When I ask her 'Why?!' she'll always respond, 'It's just so unusual and sweet'. But hasn't she noticed, everyone's called that sort of thing nowadays... and anyway, who wants to sound like a Victorian virtue? Certainly not me.*

*So, I've always insisted on Stanzy. Stanzy has a ring to it... Stanzy Somerville.*

*Yes, absolutely, let's talk about Sam... I've been seeing him almost six months.*

*Sam is the man who's perfect you see... everything about him is a dream. From the places he goes to the people he's seen with, it's always guaranteed to be the right thing. Effortlessly stylish, amazingly cool, and just so good-looking! Friends often comment he looks like James Dean and I still can't believe he's chosen me!*

*When I picture Sam, as I often do, he's wearing his black leather jacket and vintage sunglasses, hair pushed back from his brow. He's laughing and everyone's laughing with him. I sometimes catch myself just gazing... Sam's certainly something to see.*

*Waiters offer him the best table and we never stand in line.*

*Even when it comes to women... endlessly circling... Sam flirts back, sure... but I'm his girlfriend, so I tell myself that and don't say a thing.*

*Half my life is spent these days sitting outside some trendy bar with bystanders glancing in Sam's direction. He's always smoking, but in that laid-back kind of way that only the cool can muster. Nothing seems to stick to him and life just glides on by. It feels like we're in a movie with Sam as the star; it's love... it has to be.*

*So why have my eyes started wandering?*

*Let me give you an example... just to show you how crazy it is!*

*We were having a drink at this bar in Brixton only the other day. To tell you the truth, I was slightly bored, I don't even know why... everything was much as usual. Sam was slouched in the chair next to mine, legs crossed over... casually. When there he was, this scruffy-looking guy... doing the Metro crossword puzzle.*

*He was wearing a pair of trainers which looked like they'd died five years ago; his jeans were torn in completely the wrong direction and he'd topped the whole disaster off with a polyester anorak!*

*'Oh my God!' I thought. 'Is he blind! What kind of a person wears an outfit like that!'*

*Sam's phone buzzed loudly, catching his attention...*

*'Hey man, how's it going?'*

*It must have been Ted... at least judging by the conversation.*

*The guy seemed intent on his crossword puzzle.*

*And then I started to fantasise.*

*Now the first thing you need to know is I'd never go out with someone like that. I just couldn't... what would people say? But his face looked warm and inviting; his eyes were soft and his hands strong. He wasn't looking from left to right as I often catch myself doing, and there was something about him that breathed contentment.*

*'I bet that guy does something really worthwhile,' I thought to myself. 'Perhaps he works for a charity, or maybe he's some kind of eco-warrior, fighting to save the planet'. The eco-warrior didn't look up.*

*Who knows how long I was dreaming... probably not that long... but Sam turned towards me at the end of the phone call, and I smiled. His eyes flicked over to the guy with the crossword puzzle, he unfurled his legs, then suggested we head off.*

*Later that night as I lay in bed, I found myself thinking about the man again... wondering what it would be like to date someone who did something so amazing! 'Oh yes... he doesn't care a thing about his appearance, he's just too committed to the cause. There isn't time and anyway it's so superficial,' I sighed.*

*Two minutes later a message came in from Sophie. 'Drinks tomorrow?'*

*Why not."*

# SAM'S TALE

*"So, what can I say about Stanzy?*

*Well, what would you like to know?*

*5' 10" with spectacular legs... her body's slender, her lips are full and her hair the perfect shade of honey blonde. Everyone comments on how great we look together... and I have to say I agree.*

*She's the sort of girl who's easy to be with... willing to give you space. Girls can often come on a bit strong and perhaps I'm not always that faithful, but Stanzy isn't the clingy type and she never tries to snoop. Essential for anyone I'm dating.*

*She's adoring, of course, but there's no suggestion of anything serious and, let's face it, that's the last thing I need at my time of life.*

*The other day some tiresome 'friend' had the nerve to suggest I settle down.*

*'Aren't you close to forty?' he smirked. I almost struck him off my contact list right there and then. What kind of a jerk says a thing like that? And anyway, I'm thirty-seven!*

*When Stanzy hits thirty I might have to dump her just to be on the safe side. The last thing I need is a woman who wants the whole child, commitment thing; it's just not my style. I'm a party guy and I don't mind admitting it.*

*So, what are you thinking?... Ah, yes, let's see... you really believe I can't guess? I can. I've heard it all before. How shallow I am... how lacking in serious intent.*

*'God! What an a\*\*hole,' I hear you half-murmuring. 'Nothing but style over substance.'*

*But, I'd like to ask you, how much do you make? Because as a 'Creative' I'm pulling in a six-figure sum. Life's pretty ok from where I'm standing; how about you?*

*Still, there's something that, somehow, I just can't grasp... can't quite put my finger on. It's neatly summed up by an odd little incident that happened the other day.*

*I'd been seeing a friend for an hour or two, about some project in Brixton. So Stanzy and I had stayed on for a drink... nothing unusual in that.*

*Anyway, opposite our table and directly in view, sat this offensively scruffy bloke. His feet were stuck in some filthy trainers and he looked like a total Anorak... which, believe it or not, was actually what he was wearing! The guy was alone... of course... and to complete the scene he was doing the Metro crossword puzzle.*

*'Christ!' I thought. 'What a loser.'*

*But Stanzy kept glancing in his direction... she was definitely curious. Curious about what? My phone buzzed shifting my attention, but I couldn't help noticing that bloke in the anorak was holding my girlfriend's gaze.*

*When I rang off I suggested we leave. Neither of us mentioned the incident... what was there to say? But something had happened, an attraction had sparked, and it isn't the first time either. I've caught other girlfriends' eyes start wandering, onto some idiot or other... but this guy was the limit! What could a loser like that have to offer anyone?! Somebody tell me."*

# WHAT'S THE GAME?

'Will You Be My Movie Star' is a very common Game, guaranteed to be played by all of us. Its central theme is projection.

---

## DEFINITION

Projection is the psychological mechanism by which we attribute to other people our own unconscious impulses and personality traits. Projection doesn't refer to those half-acknowledged characteristics we attempt to disown in ourselves but are quick to observe in others; it occurs when we have absolutely no awareness the quality in question belongs to us.

---

As the people we choose to project these traits onto will often, though not always, possess them as well, our actions remain safe from self-scrutiny and we can continue in ignorance of our true ownership.

Projection can either be positive or negative and occurs on both an individual and collective basis. When used to deny our more negative characteristics it has the capacity to create highly damaging consequences.

# COLLECTIVE PROJECTION

In its collective form projection appears most obviously within any social, political or spiritual grouping noted for its strong values and belief systems.

All groups founded on a firmly held set of ideals have to contend with the temptation of believing themselves special and different.

The more they regard their values as the only 'right' way to view the world, the harder it becomes to acknowledge and accept the failings and inconsistencies within their own collective. Once the majority succumbs to a belief in their moral or spiritual superiority, the likelihood of their own failings being projected onto other social groups is strong.

It follows that the more rigid and isolating the tenets of a group, the more common the growth of a communal attitude that outsiders are essentially wrong. A siege mentality can develop and with it a failure to recognise the groups negative impulses.

# INDIVIDUAL PROJECTION

Individuals who don't identify with a particular group or set of ideals are no more likely to escape projection's grasp.

We all have a *Shadow*. This is the collective name given to our unconscious impulses and personality traits.

What is the one characteristic you detest in others but genuinely don't believe you possess yourself? That is your strongest negative projection, hidden inside your Shadow.

Only through vigilant awareness of our personal weaknesses and a willingness to reflect on what others say about us, particularly if their comments prompt an irrationally strong reaction, can we hope to mitigate the problem.

Much that lies buried within the Shadow can with patience emerge into conscious awareness, but it requires us to hold our ideas about who we are and what we believe more lightly than is often comfortable.

The compensation for such uncertainty is the freedom which greater self-awareness offers each time we withdraw one of our projections.

## STANZY AND SAM

Stanzy and Sam are caught in their own personal projections, but they are also identified with a social and cultural grouping loosely defined as the 'cool creatives'.

They use this identification to re-enforce a belief in their superiority, a belief that is validated by the places they choose to visit and the people they see.

Stanzy: *"Waiters offer him the best table and we never stand in line."*

Consequently, Stanzy, and particularly Sam, need to conduct a carefully curated lifestyle not only in terms of social hangouts but also friends. Anyone who threatens to undermine their self-image faces the possibility of ejection.

Sam: *"I almost struck him off my contact list right there and then."*

The problems attached to this need to feel special and different should not be confused with the process all young people go through when seeking to create an identity apart from their parents. It's normal for our initial sense of self to be at least partially derived from looking outwards; we search for people whose habits, ideas and dress codes reflect how we feel about ourselves.

The collective aspect of 'Will You Be My Movie Star' appears at the point where an initial sense of identity has been formed, but because of internal and often unconscious insecurities the need to set oneself apart persists.

It is the line between a healthy sense of belonging and a need to marginalise and condemn others to feel better about oneself.

# STANZY

Stanzy is young. She's enjoying her beauty and having fun with life and why not? Life is for living. Her narrative, however, suggests that she has little idea of who she really is.

At first glance Stanzy seems self-assured. She's made a conscious effort to create her own identity and appears confident in her choices.

Stanzy: *"I've always insisted on Stanzy. Stanzy has a ring to it... Stanzy Somerville."*

But why is she so obsessed by her boyfriend's appearance and popularity? Sam not only has to look right; he must also be popular and desired.

By being part of an apparently 'golden couple', Stanzy feels validated by her chosen peer group and consequently good about herself. She's in love with the image of Sam much more than the man himself.

Stanzy: *"It feels like we're in a movie with Sam as the star."*

This points to an underlying insecurity evident in the narrative.

Stanzy: *"I still can't believe he's chosen me!"*

Insecurity is inhibiting Stanzy's exploration of other less obvious qualities that she's starting to value in a relationship, and her rather complicated attraction to the man with the Metro crossword puzzle reveals a struggle to understand her own internal longing for depth as well as glamour.

When Stanzy initially notices the man, she's baffled by her own attraction.

Stanzy: *"Now the first thing you need to know is that I'd never go out with a guy like that. I just couldn't... what would people say?"*

She has to invent a fantasy to explain her feelings: the eco-warrior saving the planet.

Stanzy: *"'I bet that guy does something really worthwhile,' I thought to myself."*

It isn't enough for Stanzy that he appears thoughtful and centred; she's too insecure to be seen with the 'wrong guy', the man who might be labelled 'ordinary' by her social group. Stanzy fears being 'ordinary' by association.

Her very act of noticing him, however, suggests she's closer than she realises to a more active search for something beyond superficial appearance.

Stanzy is projecting onto the *"eco-warrior"* a kindness and strength she's unaware of in herself. In doing so, she's demonstrating how projection can be positive as well as negative.

We can all be blind to our kinder qualities, as much as the

selfish, more venal aspects of who we are, but projection in its positive form is still a fantasy, obscuring access both to ourselves and the other person.

# SAM

Sam like Stanzy, is caught in his love of appearance. He's a physically attractive man who's found validation through apparently effortless beauty and style. It's therefore within his interests to view these qualities as being of primary importance when it comes to judging others.

An unconscious strategy we commonly employ for coping with insecurity is to choose an attribute we're acknowledged to possess: intelligence, creativity, agility, style, then denigrate others by implicit comparison to this one quality (e.g.: 'What does she look like!').

Even when this strategy is expressed using half-joking irony, it still serves to draw attention to our own superior prowess in the field:

'She's clever, it's true... but have you seen her soft furnishings!'

We feel better about ourselves.

Sam stands at the extreme end of this spectrum and those who fail to match up to his personal standards of beauty and material success are likely to meet with a negative judgement.

Sam: *"'Christ!' I thought. 'What a loser.'"*

Sam's high level of grandiosity and intolerance indicates a strong need to project his own unconscious fear of being a *"loser"* onto someone else. He has no awareness of this.

Unlike Stanzy, Sam is clear that their relationship is based on good looks. This when coupled with Stanzy's willingness to accommodate his flirtatious behaviour, appears to be the only real attraction.

Sam: *"When Stanzy hits thirty I might have to dump her just to be on the safe side."*

Stanzy herself is aware of the role Sam's movie star looks are playing, but she needs to wrap her attraction up in a confused idea of love.

Stanzy: *"it's love... it has to be."*

Stanzy is essentially looking for more; Sam is not.

# POSITIVE STEPS FOR CHANGE

Stanzy and Sam are facing quite different dilemmas.

# STANZY

Stanzy's attraction to the man with the Metro crossword puzzle suggests she's close to searching for something beyond superficial glamour. Her eyes are *"wandering"* and part of her is already trying to work out why.

Stanzy: *"There was something about him that breathed contentment."*

Stanzy is moving away from simple admiration of movie star looks and starting to see physical beauty for what it is: a pleasure to behold but not a sound quality to base a relationship on.

Whilst it's useful for Stanzy to reflect on what she really values in other people, she also needs to recognise her own capacity for strength and kindness. Right now, she's simply projecting these qualities onto someone else.

If Stanzy starts paying closer attention to what's both attracting and repelling her in others, she will start to discover the ways she's unconsciously seeking to grow.

Trying to unearth the more difficult aspects of her personality will not help Stanzy right now. As already mentioned, her dependence on Sam for validation suggests an underlying insecurity.

Stanzy: *"I still can't believe he's chosen me!"*

Any attempt to examine Stanzy's darker character traits may just send her into the negative thought spiral of 'I'm not good enough'. Her ego is too fragile for the quest.

Stanzy's search for greater meaning is far better served by reflecting on her own positive projections. Good friends can be helpful in pointing out qualities she may not recognise in herself.

When Stanzy starts to see she is more than the good-looking girl with the sense of style, she'll begin to choose men of more substance.

It's unlikely she'll make the quantum leap to the scruffy guy in the anorak; a trendy exterior will continue to matter. It will, however, be placed in proper perspective.

# SAM

Sam's in a different position to Stanzy. He's aware he's judged by others, but on the surface appears not to care.

Sam: *"So, what are you thinking? Ah, yes, let's see... you really believe I can't guess? I can. I've heard it all before [...] But, I'd like to ask you... how much do you make? Because as a 'Creative' I'm pulling in a six-figure sum. Life's pretty ok from where I'm standing; how about you?"*

Sam chooses to view any personal criticism as envy of his material success and he may in part be right. But his attitude is also a defence mechanism, serving to protect him from having to reflect on his own behaviour.

Sam's arrogant contempt and easy willingness to sneer at others makes him an easy target for our own negative projections. In choosing to judge him, however, all we are doing is unconsciously offloading our own arrogance and insecurity onto someone else: look at him; thank God I'm not like that.

Such judgement is ultimately counterproductive. Sam will respond defensively and become more, not less entrenched in his attitudes. So, whilst we may feel better on a temporary basis, both we and Sam will continue to sit in easy judgement on others, with no one fundamentally served.

The longer Sam continues down his current path, the harder it's going to be to change. If he's materially successful Sam will continue to attract people willing to validate him in return for the glamour that money and style can bring. If he's not, then as his looks and fortune fade his lifestyle will likewise decline, and the edifice upon which he's built his self-worth will start to crumble. Sam will then be in danger of descending into an uncomprehending and oddly self-righteous bitterness, castigating others for the very contempt he previously demonstrated.

What Sam needs is to surround himself with people who value him for more than simply money and looks. A tall order given his attitude.

If he's fortunate enough to attract such people, their willingness to see his more positive qualities will enable Sam to discover them himself, and this will start to modify his behaviour.

Negative criticism is only possible when a strong bond of caring and trust has developed between Sam and his critic.

Sam's biggest problem is that as things currently stand he's unlikely to be able to rescue himself, or even recognise his need for help.

# EPILOGUE

## STANZY

*"The other evening, quite by chance, I bumped into someone from school. Clara and I were strolling through the foyer when we saw her... Shola Daramola, the queen of 3b. She was heading purposefully towards the box office... our destination. So no avoiding her then. Shola had reigned at the top of our class – brains as well as beauty – and as we stood in the queue behind her back we both fell silent.*

*Clara was probably waiting for the clever put-down... I know I was. Our school had been pretty brutal when it came to low achievers. But the put-down never came. Instead, Shola actually offered me a compliment! At least I think she did.*

*'You're not going to believe this,' she said, 'but I always rather admired you at school. You had this way of saying just the right thing whenever a friend was upset. Do you remember Katie Cunningham crying over that stupid boy? God, it was endless! I just stood there not knowing what to do. Then you swept in with an enormous hug and the absolute assurance she was worth more! I'll never forget it; it's quite a gift, you know.'*

*Shola headed off to the popcorn stand and Clara turned to me and smiled.*

*'Who'd have guessed it! Superstar Shola offers a compliment. You deserve it, darling.'*

*Do I? I've never actually thought of a comforting hug as being a talent. Well, if it is, it's certainly something Sam doesn't possess. Sometimes I think it would be nice to date someone just a little bit warmer.*

*The man with the Metro crossword puzzle slid into my mind. We turned to the girl behind the counter and bought two tickets. Clara squeezed my arm and we strolled in."*

# SAM

*"It's just not working with Stanzy any more and I've no idea what's happened.*

*We were at some party of a friend's last night and she didn't even look at me once!*

*Instead she sat lounging on Brad's stupid sofa, chatting to a guy who looked like Brains from Thunderbirds! I asked Brad who he was... I guess I just had to know. Apparently, his name's Johnny. Johnny spends his time slaving for Google and judging by what he was wearing they certainly don't discriminate against the 'fashionably challenged'. Stanzy was smiling, laughing and looking so happy! I know I like my space but – Christ! – what makes her think I want to watch her flirt!*

*Her WhatsApp messages have fallen off a cliff and when I asked her to come over late last night she just said she couldn't make it.*

*Fine... suits me. She's pretty it's true, but honestly that's about it. In fact, when I stop to think about it, Stanzy's vanity is really quite breathtaking. It's amazing how some people have a completely inflated opinion of their own self-importance.*

*There are so many beautiful girls out there... and, let's face it, plenty more interested in me... I only have to flash them a smile. She'll learn."*

# WHAT'S LOVE GOT TO DO WITH IT?

## THE TALE OF EDIE AND MAX

# MAX'S TALE

"Have I mentioned my girlfriend, Edie Everdene? I have? Yes, I must have done... she's constantly on my mind.

We met six months ago, at one of Hope's parties... and from the very beginning I was smitten. Spirited and beautiful with an easy grace and sparkling wit, no one could take their eyes off her. The following day, when I rang to say thank you, I couldn't help asking for her number. We've been together ever since.

There's nothing that Edie isn't curious to explore... art, poetry, music, dancing... it's thrilling to be with her. I feel so alive!

But, try as I might, I can't pin her down and any attempt to take our relationship forward gets me nowhere. She's happy to jump in my ridiculous sports car and speed off for a country house break, and she's constantly telling me how great I am... how much she loves being in my company. But her friends seem to take up too much of her time and her job has considerably more corporate entertainment than I've ever heard of.

To be frank it's driving me mad! Whenever a message pops up on my phone, my stomach lurches forward in case it's from her. I can't eat, I can't sleep and I'm stupidly nervous... it feels like a sickness I just can't cure.

I've even started worrying that she's seeing other men...

*friends have hinted as much, although I doubt it's true. But even if it is... what can I do? Edie's never offered commitment so how can I challenge her? She'd say I was asking for something she's just not ready to give. So, I don't... I don't want to lose all that energy and brilliance. Any time with Edie is so much better than none.*

*The other day David called at the weekend... to ask if I felt like meeting for a drink. We were having a pleasant enough pint at this pub off the Heath but when I mentioned Edie things became decidedly awkward. Yes, she was beautiful but what a firecracker! He started going on about all the great-looking girls just longing to go out with me... of everything I have to offer the right woman... how lucky she'd be. Is he mad! Hasn't he any idea of my feelings for Edie?*

*I'm certain Hope put him up to it, David would never voluntarily interfere in another man's love life, but, even so, his complete inability to recognise what makes her special was massively annoying.*

*Then just when I thought the subject was closed he started to comment on my love life in general!... why did I always go for unavailable girls?*

*What is he?... my therapist?! What I want to know is, why is it everyone feels they have the right to express their ill-informed opinions at the slightest opportunity?*

*Yes, it's true, I do go for girls who are so beautiful and full of life they just aren't ready to settle down, but why wouldn't a man go for all that energy and pizzazz! If I could have gone further with any of them I would... in fact, I've tried to on more than one occasion. And, as for Edie, I've been hit so hard I'd give my right arm for commitment.*

*Love is a drug... amazing and horrifying. But this time I'm left wondering exactly where it's going to end?*

*I'll be forty-two next year and last summer I found myself tempted into buying this beautiful townhouse. It has a sixty-foot garden with a well-kept lawn and an oak tree just perfect for a swing. So, something in me is definitely hankering to settle down and part of me hopes Edie might yet be persuaded. She's certainly enchanting, but there's something special there too... a sensitivity and compassion that draws me on. I'm not giving up yet."*

# EDIE'S TALE

*"Max is brilliant. I mean literally brilliant. He's some sort of analyst at a city bank... earning pots and with super prospects. All my friends say I'd be mad to let him slip through my fingers and when I think about it logically I have to agree.*

*We met through Hope, at one of her parties... about six months ago now. Hope and I go back a long way. We went to school together, plus university, then finally to London, looking for fun. It feels like a lifetime ago. But her world has contracted into an endless round of school runs and 'what little Johnny did last weekend', so I was there to entertain... she made no bones about that.*

*Max in particular seemed quite captivated, so when he rang the next day I wasn't surprised. Apparently, Hope had given him my number and as we'd been the only single people at dinner I'd already suspected a set-up. It would be typical of Hope to take on the challenge... although, judging by what I've heard recently, she's regretting her decision. People do love to interfere don't they... what has our relationship got to do with her?*

*Anyway... Max. Max is the man that all the girls long for, he's thoughtful and clever and surprisingly witty. So, although the sex is far from amazing and the sports car a bit of an overcompensation, being with him can really be fun.*

*But there's something so very off-putting about someone who's clearly smitten, particularly if I'm honest when I'm not that smitten myself. My life seems full of situations where I'm expected to add a touch of glamour and excitement to proceedings... so of course that's what I do. But it feels as if Max is expecting that glamorous party girl on pretty much a full-time basis and quite frankly it just isn't possible.*

*He's pressing for greater commitment and part of me knows it's time to settle down, but the thought of being the perfect mother and hostess for the next forty years is enough to make me run for the hills. I'm afraid I'll start to kick against it. When I look at Max's house and his picture-book garden I can almost see the two children and the endless dinner parties, as the man with the crush on the 'bright free spirit' tries to shoehorn me into domesticity.*

*He suspects me of seeing other men, at least that's the impression his endless questioning gives, and I wonder if 'friends' have been talking behind my back, but technically it isn't true; I just like to run around a little. I need to feel alive.*

*Closeness of any kind invariably ends up feeling suffocating and I've learnt it's best avoided.*

*Yet here I am going out with him and here he is going out with me. There are plenty of girls in London who'd give their right arm to go out with a man like Max and are longing to settle down. Not to mention an equal number of guys all too happy to offer zero security or commitment... and I know it. I know how lucky I am. I even really like him, and I certainly don't want to take advantage just for my own material gain.*

*So, is it right to settle for a man who offers security when I'm not certain how I feel? Or will our differences in character and expectation just make us both unhappy? I guess the real question is: what do we both want and need?"*

# WHAT'S THE GAME?

'What's Love Got to Do with It?' has more than one theme, but the question that lies at the heart of its narrative is *what is the nature of romantic love?*

## MAX

What's most immediately striking when listening to Max is the strength of his romantic projections.

Max is projecting his own unrealised needs and fantasies onto Edie and imagining everything he longs for can be found in her.

---

### DEFINITION

Projection is the psychological mechanism by which we attribute to other people our own unconscious impulses and personality traits. Projection doesn't refer to those half-acknowledged characteristics we attempt to disown in ourselves but are quick to observe in others; it occurs when we have absolutely no awareness the quality in question belongs to us.

---

Whilst it's often associated with an unconscious desire to deny our more negative impulses, projection can also encompass those qualities we most admire.

Max is projecting his unmet need for freedom, excitement and adventure onto Edie.

Max: *"There's nothing that Edie isn't curious to explore... art, poetry, music, dancing... it's thrilling to be with her. I feel so alive!"*

Edie is probably by nature freer-spirited and more adventurous than Max, but he'd be unable to recognise these qualities in her if they weren't likewise dormant in him.

Given his occupation and sense of responsibility, Max may have an unconscious fear of allowing his desire for freedom to find its true expression, and in many ways it's safer and more convenient to be involved with a woman who can express this feeling on his behalf.

The attitudes and expectations that Max and Edie demonstrate, fall into the stereotypical gender roles of the financially secure and stable man and the woman who's there to please him.

Max has been here before.

Max: *"Yes, it's true, I do go for girls who are so beautiful and full of life they just aren't ready to settle down.*

Max is caught in the repetitive cycle of pursuing free-spirited and essentially unavailable women.

To explore this repetitive pattern, we need to return to attachment theory, previously discussed in 'Such a Sweety', but first let's look at Max's experience from the perspective of romantic love.

So, what is romantic love? How can we differentiate it from infatuation? And how do the two experiences relate to one another?

* *Romantic love* is a profound recognition of the extraordinary qualities we glimpse in the being of the other.
* *Infatuation* by contrast is essentially about ourselves.

*Infatuation* is centred on the certain desire and unlikely belief that someone can make us 'whole' and results in a highly unrealistic expectation of what that person is capable of and how far they can determine our future happiness.

If we're infatuated with someone we think of them constantly, so can easily fool ourselves into imagining we wish the fulfilment of their private desires. The reality, however, is very different. Because we exaggerate their power to determine our future well-being, we will discourage any need in them which would leave us feeling separation, disappointment or lack.

They are the object of our subjective desire and as such they're personal needs are entirely subordinate to our own. Any conflict that arises with our need to keep them close cannot be countenanced or even acknowledged.

In order internally to square the circle between professing love and acting out of self-interest, we often persuade ourselves we only have our lover's best interests at heart when seeking to discourage them from something which doesn't serve us.

It's perfectly natural to pursue our own needs and life works best in an atmosphere of mutual reciprocity but, because we imagine our needs can only be met through intimate involvement

with another, we essentially play a confidence trick on ourselves by denying our true motivations.

*Romantic love* by contrast has at its heart the capacity for an extraordinary level of self-sacrifice.

For the first few months, the difficult, jaded and more cynical aspects of the beloved dissolve in the eyes of the lover and if circumstance demands, the lover is often prepared to forgo their own needs for the good of the beloved.

When both parties possess such feelings simultaneously it's one of the most magical experiences we can have, but our admiration will inevitably become grounded in the reality of an imperfect world. As familiarity grows, our beloved must be recognised and acknowledged with all their fears and imperfections, as we recognise our own inadequacies.

And here we come to the central paradox. Romantic love and infatuation stand at opposite ends of our emotional spectrum, but as they draw closer and start to mingle their purpose is revealed as the same:

To ensure our survival, we all possess a healthy amount of self-interest, and this includes an awareness that the needs of our partner, children, family and tribe are intrinsically interwoven with our own ability to survive. As such, we are often willing to put their needs before our personal desires and this creates an emotional landscape defined by complexity, nuance and doubt.

The balance we strike between blatant self-interest and the subtler self-preservation of altruism is essentially mirrored in the balance our psyche unconsciously strives for between romantic love and infatuation. What matters therefore in a romantic encounter is where that balance lies.

If the primary feeling is infatuation, then the emotional outcome will be a difficult one. As the love object's character is more fully revealed, our fantasy of perfect happiness is replaced by a growing sense of disappointment. They have failed to meet our expectations, either through wilful disregard or by proving themselves incapable, and we become increasingly disillusioned. The more extreme the infatuation, the more likely the person once doted upon now becomes the object of our rage.

Romantic love will also carry its tinge of disappointment. It's rare we experience this profound emotion without also experiencing the fantasy of complete personal fulfilment. Self-interest in fact is an important component, as it prevents the possibility of too great a self-sacrifice.

In contrast, however, with infatuation, as the difficult aspects of our beloved become apparent, disillusionment is replaced with acceptance. A more mature love for the person develops, one which recognises them as a flawed human being.

Acceptance and empathy trump self-regard in the pursuit of personal happiness.

Max is certainly demonstrating many of the hallmarks of infatuation and Edie is right in imagining he'll expect her to express the vivacity, charm and free spirit he has yet to discover in himself. But Max is aware that Edie is more than simply the perfect party girl.

Max: *"She's certainly enchanting, but there's something special there too... a sensitivity and compassion that draws me on."*

He's right. Edie is displaying greater delicacy of feeling when it comes to Max's needs than he's presently capable of experiencing for her. He has recognised her underlying kindness.

Edie: *"I know how lucky I am. I even really like him and certainly don't want to take advantage just for my own material gain... I guess the real question is: What do we both want and need?"*

Although Max is primarily bound up in his own needs, compulsions and projections, when it comes to love versus infatuation the situation isn't entirely hopeless. There is the possibility of Max accepting Edie for who she really is once his fantasies start to subside.

So now we come to the other difficulty Max and Edie are facing.

Edie is not in love with Max.

Max is too invested in the outcome to allow this awareness to fully express itself in his conscious mind, but it hangs around the corners and troubles him.

Max: *"Any attempt to take our relationship forward gets me nowhere."*

This lack of reciprocity creates an emotional imbalance at the heart of the relationship, which whilst it may shift over time cannot be considered a good beginning.

Separate but connected to Edie's reticence, are the problems attendant upon Max and Edie's shared attachment style. This time we aren't witnessing the dance of the avoidant and ambivalent, as we saw in 'Such a Sweety', but the subtler and less obvious juxtaposition of two avoidants together. This returns us to the question already posed: why is Max repeatedly pursuing free-spirited and essentially unavailable women?

Max is pursuing unavailable women because on an unconscious level he's seeking to avoid emotional intimacy, not embrace it. This avoidance is masked both to himself and others, by the fact that he has no conscious awareness of what's happening. Max believes he wants nothing more than love and emotional commitment, despite consistently accomplishing the reverse.

Max has an avoidant attachment style as outlined in attachment theory.

# ATTACHMENT THEORY

### DEFINITION

Attachment theory is a theoretical model that takes as its focus the relationship formed between a child and their primary caregiver. The attachment style we develop as children is a key contributor to how we relate in adult life.

A *secure attachment* is able to grow when the parental figure responds with a high degree of care and consistency to a child's needs. Their warmth and love engender trust, resulting in an atmosphere of safety and explorative play.

A straightforward and loving relationship in childhood translates into a secure sense of self as an adult and a willingness to take emotional risks without a crippling sense of doubt.

Difficult circumstances or fractured parenting, however, often fail to create a sufficiently safe environment for a secure attachment to form. When this occurs one of three attachment styles will develop:

At the extreme end of the spectrum sits *disorganised attachment*, reserved for those whose parenting has proved wholly inadequate. For the purposes of this book, however, I wish to stay within the realm of commonly experienced difficulties.

The two broad categories left are: the *anxious ambivalent* and the *anxious avoidant*.

In 'Such a Sweety' we explored ambivalent attachment through analysis of the character of Joe. This problem is most often created by an unpredictable level of responsiveness in the primary caregiver, sometimes loving and receptive but too often insensitive and unavailable. The resulting uncertainty and confusion fostered are carried forward into relationships in adult life.

Whilst Max's hot pursuit might initially suggest an anxious ambivalent attachment style, what differentiates him from the character of Joe is that Edie doesn't experience him as overbearingly needy. Excessive neediness is one of the most common characteristics of the anxious ambivalent and the principal focus of Lucy's complaints about Joe. Edie makes no such complaint about Max.

I refer the reader back to 'Such a Sweety' for further exploration of anxious ambivalence, as the focus for this chapter will be the avoidant.

# THE AVOIDANT

Both Edie and Max fall into the category of avoidant, but as already noted Max's avoidance is more complex than Edie's.

Avoidant attachment develops when an infant experiences their primary caregiver as essentially unresponsive to their needs. This fosters the belief that it's better to avoid seeking comfort, as expressions of need will lead to rejection.

Avoidant attachment style can be subdivided into different categories, but the fundamental theme is always the same: the avoidant adult will shy away from expressing emotional vulnerability out of a conscious or unconscious assumption that any expression of need will lead to rejection, disappointment and pain.

One of the primary reasons why Max has unconsciously chosen a woman who's not in love with him is because it protects him from the possibility of true emotional intimacy, an alien and frightening experience for Max. It would be interesting to observe his reaction if Edie started to respond more fully and began to fall in love.

Max is a man who flirts with freedom but essentially values safety. What could be safer than the unconscious awareness you will never have to confront your most deep-seated emotional fears.

Yet Max is experiencing intense and visceral feelings. How could he ever guess that his own unconscious driver is to avoid intimacy, not embrace it? It's the perfect set-up to keep awareness from his conscious mind.

'What's Love Got to Do with It?' contains a very subtle form of intimacy avoidance. One of the participants will always experience extreme emotion yet, because there's no reciprocity, on a more profound level they will ultimately remain safe.

Becoming emotionally vulnerable to someone willing to reciprocate, is both exhilarating and terrifying; for in experiencing

true union we must also accept the possibility of profound loss. Unrequited love whilst often accompanied by intense suffering precludes the possibility of abandonment, for both parties were never truly together.

# EDIE

Edie's avoidance stands in plain sight.

Edie: *"Closeness of any kind invariably ends up feeling suffocating and I've learnt it's best avoided."*

Under different circumstances and with other people, however, Max and Edie's positions could be reversed.

It's unclear from the narrative whether Edie has consistently been the obvious avoidant or if she's also experienced what it's like to be in Max's shoes.

Edie: *"There are plenty of girls in London who'd give their right arm to go out with a man like Max and are longing to settle down. Not to mention an equal number of guys all too happy to offer zero security and commitment... and I know it."*

Whilst a repetitive pattern will often follow the same format (e.g. the man who repeatedly chases unavailable women), there are those amongst us who are equally stuck, but unconsciously act out their pattern in a variety of ways:

If we take an imaginative leap into Edie's past, here are the possibilities:

1.  Previously it was Edie who fell for a dashing avoidant. He swept her off her feet then dumped her like a ton of bricks. She was left in a state of painful unrequited love but still safe from intimacy.

2.  Edie became involved with a string of superficially different people (e.g. a sensible solicitor, followed by an impoverished artist) but the underlying dynamic remained the same: avoidance.

If we express our attachment style in a variety of ways, we can easily be seduced into believing our relationship choices are varied, when in fact they're always the same.

In 'Such a Sweety', Joe's ability to have good female friends illustrates how the level of intimacy required for friendship is often more comfortable for someone struggling with attachment difficulties Over time, a person with an avoidant attachment style might decide the feelings required for friendship are as far as they're able to go. When this happens, what appears to be romantic involvement, is actually friendship.

# POSITIVE STEPS FOR CHANGE

# MAX

Max more than Edie is in danger of disappointment.

The heady mixture of romantic love and infatuation he's currently experiencing is not reciprocated, and on some level, Max is aware of this.

One of the questions Max needs to ask himself is: what would it be like to marry a woman knowing she doesn't feel the same way about me?

Whilst this isn't currently crossing his mind, if he succeeds in persuading Edie to marry him it will increasingly impinge on his consciousness.

When David asks Max why he pursues unavailable women he dismisses the question out of hand. This suggests that Max is unwilling to engage in honest self-reflection. Yet, if the relationship is to stand any chance of success he needs to look at this aspect of himself.

Unless Max is willing to address his own avoidance he's in very real danger of marrying Edie only to experience one of three outcomes:

1. If the dominant feeling is infatuation then five years later, when Edie fails to live up to Max's expectations, his eye will be drawn to the next great conquest, imagining this time it's 'real'. Dependent on the strength of this new infatuation Max will either divorce or embark on an affair.

2. Max's feelings of romantic love keep him true to Edie, but he spends his marriage pursuing a wife for a love, that not only she can't give, but which he fundamentally cannot receive.

3. Edie tries to conquer her own avoidance and seeks a greater level of intimacy with Max, but he finds himself incapable of receiving her love and starts to pull away.

Max is in the grip of very powerful feelings and will doggedly pursue his goal of matrimony regardless of what anyone says. If Edie consents they will marry.

Fortunately, however, the possibility for self-awareness and change remain, even if the marriage has a bumpy beginning.

If Max can recognise his own avoidance, then a window of opportunity is opened to explore his fear of intimacy.

Max is aware of Edie's kindness. Her curiosity, compassion and sensitivity will still be present as his projections start to fade; he will continue to care for her. Acknowledgement of his own unconscious complicity in avoidance will help spare Max the fruitless pursuit of a wife too scared to love him and allow them the chance to address their attachment difficulties together.

This is the beacon of hope in an otherwise unpromising situation, but it requires that Edie be likewise willing to engage.

# EDIE

Edie isn't in love with Max and, as such, is only too aware of the pitfalls. She imagines Max is consumed by her glamour and knows it isn't real.

Edie: *"It feels as if Max is expecting that glamorous party girl on pretty much a full-time basis and quite frankly it just isn't possible."*

Max, however, is drawn to Edie's curiosity and life force as much as her capacity to enchant; Edie just can't see this. The insecurities engendered by emotional abandonment mean she's used to relating to men in a superficial manner: why allow them too close? They probably won't like what they see.

But Max does like what he sees. If Edie can recognise that Max's feelings are based on her intrinsic qualities as much as her superficial glamour, not only will it be a personally healing experience; it will draw them closer together.

Edie also needs to start focusing on Max's intrinsic qualities. At present his desire is dominating the discourse, making it difficult for either of them to concentrate on what's meaningful. Edie describes Max as thoughtful, clever and witty: she genuinely likes him.

So, is Edie prepared to curtail her freedom? And how far can she cope with recognition of Max's love?

Edie's belief that Max wishes to crush her *"bright free spirit"* reflects her own fears far more than Max's fantasy. She's right however in assuming that she, far more than he, will have to compromise her lifestyle. Yet there's obviously a part of Edie longing for security and commitment or she wouldn't be with Max at all.

Edie admires Max's many qualities and it's possible to address her concerns without completely jeopardising their relationship.

If Edie can acknowledge her fear of not feeling good enough and see that Max is in love with her, then the situation has hope. She's unlikely to immediately overwhelm Max with emotional proximity and change is incrementally possible.

There's often a moment of realisation – the ah hah! revelation of the previously misunderstood – but our world doesn't radically shift at that point. Max and Edie could over time take baby steps towards true closeness.

The fact that Edie isn't currently in love with Max would to the romantic idealist be the toll of doom, but a mature love unclouded by infatuation can grow from admiration and care.

Intimacy and understanding can be achieved through a mutual willingness to reveal one's true nature. The power of being seen by another cannot be underestimated. What else is intimacy if not that.

# EPILOGUE

## MAX

*"In an odd sort of way it feels like a lifetime ago now, but, yes, we did get married.*

*The house is still beautiful... as is Edie... and we have the most adorable little baby girl, Elizabeth. Edie's a wonderful mother... so very kind... but when I look across at my wife these days I'm no longer sure what I was hoping for.*

*I'd managed to get myself so worked up, it's almost as if I was another person, and of course life isn't the rollercoaster ride I'd imagined... how could it be with the domestic routine of a tiny child? But isn't family life exactly what I said I wanted?*

*David came around with Hope and the boys last Sunday. God, what a racket! It immediately set the baby off. Edie of course handled it with perfect grace. She seems to have adapted seamlessly to her new situation and in many ways appears happier than me.*

*Still possessed of that wonderful curiosity for life; she fits her interests round Beth's routine... our daughter comes first for both of us. But I hanker for greater emotional intimacy and sometimes it feels as if I'm on the outside looking in. Oddly, though, whenever*

*Edie tries to come closer... an unsolicited touch on the hand or a gentle brush of my cheek... it's almost unbearably painful. I don't understand what I'm feeling myself.*

*Sometimes in the evening when Edie's curled up on the sofa reading a book I look over at her and she smiles. Our relationship certainly isn't without love and I know she cares for me. Perhaps I'm the one that's holding back, now that the madness is over... but I do so long for more."*

# EDIE

*"I thought about marriage long and hard as I knew there'd be no turning back... I didn't want there to be... and I can honestly say I'm happy with the decision I made.*

*Motherhood has given me so much more than I ever anticipated, and Max is a wonderful father. Perhaps a little distant at times, but when Beth smiles he seems to light up from within.*

*I decided if we were going to get married then I'd try to dismantle some of my emotional barricades. We are a family now and I'm determined our baby isn't going to grow up in a household dominated by silence.*

*But after all the ardour of Max's love, in a way he seems strangely reticent. If I try to get close it feels like he's pulling away and I'm no longer sure what he imagined our life would be. I've certainly altered my own way of being and from the outside we're the picture-book family he longed for. Hope commented on it the other day.*

*Maybe Max just didn't know what he was looking for himself, but perhaps over time we can find a way to grow together. I certainly hope so."*

# THE ART OF GIVING

## THE TALE OF LARA AND JAY

# LARA'S TALE

*"I first met Jay really quite by chance, at a lecture in my local arts venue. He was sitting in the front row, clearly at ease, and during the Q and As asked such piercing questions I'm not even sure the panel knew quite how to answer them.*

*I would never have gone to the talk on my own, but an old friend from college had dragged me along and I ended up really enjoying myself.*

*We decided to stay on for a quick drink afterwards and much to our excitement found ourselves standing in the queue next to Jay. Shireen struck up a conversation and invited him to share our table, but it was my number he asked for as he went to leave.*

*Jay was living in Stoke Newington at the time, in this chaotic sort of house share... just him and a couple. But no one seemed to appreciate his need for space and the whole situation was starting to get on his nerves.*

*Jay's a writer; he's had work published and is hugely talented, so it was clear he needed a place where he could focus, and I was happy to be the person able to offer him that. To be honest I was flattered he took me seriously; the last guy I'd been with was vile. Ed drank too much and ended up treating me like rubbish... yet here was Jay, actually wanting to move in!*

*At first it was amazing. Jay always acts with such conviction; whether it's listening to music, cooking a meal or making love, he's totally into it, totally there. But we've been together for over a year now and I've started to realise I'm always the one who's having to cope with everything.*

*I work full-time and the hours can be long, but when I get home at the end of the day, nothing is ever done. I used to have a lodger who helped pay the mortgage, but Claire had to go... Jay needed her room to write.*

*Along with the lodger went the money for a cleaner and Jay's not the kind of guy who'd ever clean up. He used to cook occasionally, and the meals were always incredible – although the kitchen was a total mess afterwards – but he doesn't even bother doing that anymore and, as for the bills, they've always been down to me.*

*Jay's first book was published two years before we met and to be honest it wasn't a success. He's really struggling with the second, so I've suggested he do a bit of freelancing to earn some money. At first, he said he'd ask around but now he just gets angry, accusing me of failing to understand his vision. It's true, I'm not creative and really admire people who are. The bills still need to be paid, though, and I'm starting to feel exhausted.*

*Jay's moods are getting worse as well. I often come home from a hard day's work and he's just sitting there, hunched over his laptop... daring me to break the silence. I don't. Instead I collect up the coffee cups, tiptoe into the kitchen and start cooking dinner. If things have gone well he'll talk... telling me how he's feeling and what he's trying to achieve. If they haven't, the silence continues. Then he'll go into the living room and start playing music loudly. I've had complaints from neighbours and have tried* to explain what he's going through, but they don't seem to care. If I ask him to turn it down, he loses his temper and I end up feeling guilty for suggesting it... everything seems to be about managing his moods.

In fact, everything's about Jay. Sometimes I feel so defeated I start to cry and for five minutes he's kind. But you can be guaranteed it won't last long and he'll end up in an even worse mood than before.

The irony is I just want to make him happy, but however hard I try nothing seems to be good enough. I'm starting to feel so depressed. I rarely see friends, life just feels too exhausting... and anyway if I get back late there's always a barrage of questions about where I've been. Perhaps he's right: I shouldn't be going out when he needs me. We occasionally go out together, but if he can't face it we cancel, and I can tell people are getting pissed off. Jay goes out without me quite often... to visit people of 'like mind'. What's my mind like? It's completely demoralising.

A couple of my girlfriends are starting to become quite vociferous about what they see as Jay's shortcomings and the other day Ginny told me she thinks I should throw him out! If she keeps on saying it I'm going to have to stop seeing her, she just doesn't seem to understand what he's up against or how much I care about him.

At the end of the day, I know this guy needs me. He really has an amazing talent and, anyway, what am I supposed to do? I can't throw him out: what kind of a person would that make me? In many ways I've never felt that good about myself. Taking care of Jay and trying to help him fulfil his dreams really seems worthwhile. In fact, I'm quite scared he'll leave me."

# JAY'S TALE

*"Don't get me wrong, Lara's a sweet girl... but, Christ, it's difficult! And sometimes I wonder what I'm still dong with her.*

*We met at some talk in this tiresome little arts place... standing in the queue for a drink. I spotted immediately that Lara's the type of girl who likes to take care of people and it's nice to have someone making sure the small stuff is dealt with.*

*I'd written this book, which whilst not a huge financial success had certainly had some very favourable reviews... and was living with Nick and his girlfriend at his house in Stoke Newington, but things were starting to turn sour. Nick's cool about things... Liddy, however... All she ever does is nag! I've no idea how he puts up with it; I certainly couldn't tolerate living with her. The fuss she makes about shitty little things like housework, you wouldn't believe it.*

*Then in stepped Lara, sweet-natured, attentive and kind.*

*She owns this flat in Finsbury Park, which once she'd got rid of the lodger was fine.*

*Lara seemed to genuinely appreciate my creative vision. She didn't understand it, of course, very few people do, but it felt like I'd found a place where I could completely focus on what mattered.*

*Just like every situation I've ever been involved in, though, it's starting to feel like a drag. The creative process can be tortuous, and I spend days when nothing comes, but if ever an idea is finally emerging you can be guaranteed Lara will start tapping on the door! It's always some excuse, about making me a cup of tea, but I know she just wants attention.*

*She certainly didn't come across as needy when I first met her, but, let me tell you, she is. Her attention-seeking is always wrapped up in the guise of wanting to help, asking me about my work or if I need anything... when she knows d\*mn well that what I really need is to be left alone.*

*I'm the kind of guy that when I'm with a girl it's 100%, but women seem to expect that all the time! How?! Do they think I don't want any time to myself? How am I supposed to write? The flat's always a mess, so why doesn't she throw some energy into cleaning that up instead of constantly bothering me!*

*I could write whilst she's at work, it's true, but that offers less time than you'd imagine. I'm rarely up before midday... I struggle to sleep... and even when I eventually manage to surface, it takes a couple of hours to get my head together.*

*You can be certain, however, that on the rare occasions when I do need a bit of attention she'll be out with her friends. Has she got a sixth sense or what!*

*She also refuses to act as a buffer between me and the rest of the world. Music is hugely important to me and Lara knows that, but she's constantly asking me to turn it down. Apparently, the neighbours complain. So what! Can't she deal with it?*

*Sometimes I feel so exasperated that I start shouting at her. She crumples into the corner like a little rag doll and I end up feeling guilty and trying to make it up. Then I just feel even more enraged at constantly having to attend to her needs! What about mine?!*

*In many ways I know it's time to leave. I'm just not sure where to go. Cash is tight right now and whilst I could get some freelance work it probably wouldn't pay enough.*

*Part of me is aware how dependent I've become on Lara and I'm starting to feel quite trapped. I know it suits her to have me in this position... after all, what a great way to keep control. No wonder I'm resentful!*

*Lara always portrays herself as the victim, tip toeing around the place, cooking me meals; but let me tell you, I feel pretty victimised myself... smothered by her attention and need."*

# WHAT'S THE GAME?

'The Art of Giving' is a difficult but important Game. It illustrates an issue often found in dysfunctional relationships, that of co-dependency.

Co-dependent relationships come in different guises, but they always possess this defining characteristic:

---

### DEFINITION

A co-dependent relationship exists when the needs of one person are subordinated to caring for and attempting to contain the behaviour of the other.

---

Co-dependency doesn't refer to the normal level of compassion and care mutually given in a healthy relationship. It is a corrosive pattern of behaviour that frequently worsens as time goes by.

A person who is co-dependent can only find a sense of self-worth through caring for another. It isn't enough simply to be themselves; they must be in a relationship with someone who's dependent on them to feel ok.

This often unconscious striving for self-worth is what enables

the co-dependent to tolerate the disinterest their partner generally displays, when it comes to the co-dependent's own feelings and needs.

Co-dependents have the capacity to form relationships with people caught at the extreme end of addiction; the problem was first identified in the partners of alcoholics.

Co-dependency is never a good thing. Even if on the surface the person cared for appears actively helped, the unconscious investment each party has in maintaining the status quo will inevitably keep both trapped in a destructive cycle of behaviour.

Lara and Jay do not stand at the extreme end of the spectrum. Their situation, however, is striking enough to clearly illustrate the progressive nature of the problem.

# LARA

Throughout her account it's clear Lara suffers from low self-esteem.

Her narrative indicates repetition compulsion, previously outlined in 'Come On In'.

---

### DEFINITION

Repetition compulsion is the unconscious desire to compulsively repeat a painful relationship pattern and/or early life trauma. The longing is always for a different outcome, but because the compulsive behaviour creates the same emotional dynamic, instead of resolution the original experience is simply repeated.

---

Lara: *"To be honest I was flattered he took me seriously; the last guy I'd been with was vile. Ed drank too much and ended up treating me like rubbish... yet here was Jay, actually wanting to move in!"*

As with all repetitive patterns, Lara enters the relationship hopeful of a different outcome. From the outset, however, she tolerates an unfair division of financial obligation and domestic labour, signalling to Jay that she doesn't consider herself his equal and allowing him to take advantage of her.

In trying to care for and nurture Jay's talent, Lara is attempting to vicariously gain a sense of self-worth through him. Yet the more she gives the more he's taking.

This endless giving is further compounded by her over-developed sense of responsibility towards Jay, another common symptom of co-dependency. A strong sense of responsibility can sometimes mask an underlying fear of abandonment and this is true of Lara.

Lara: *"He really has an amazing talent and, anyway, what am I supposed to do? I can't throw him out: what kind of a person would that make me?... In fact, I'm quite scared he'll leave me."*

Because she's seeking to gain Jay's approval, Lara shies away from confrontation or criticism of him. She believes her feelings are of less importance, so a sense of guilt is easily engendered if she stands up for herself.

Lara: *"Perhaps he's right: I shouldn't be going out when he needs me."*

Lara not only cares for Jay; she's also increasingly rescuing him from his own financial incompetence. She's aware of her need to be needed and this is driving her willingness to marginalise her own exhaustion and pain.

Lara: *"At the end of the day, I know this guy needs me."*

Within many relationships there's often a degree of co-dependency. We all have insecurities and a need to be needed is part of the human condition. Lara, however, stands as an example of how a situation can reach a point where it becomes emotionally abusive.

# JAY

Jay's relationship with Lara is centred on his own self-gratification and sense of personal importance, yet he appears completely unaware of this. As such, he's demonstrating in attitude and behaviour a degree of selfishness that borders on narcissism.

*Narcissism* is characterised by a grandiose sense of self-importance and an inability to identify with the feelings or needs of others. Exploitation of people for personal gain is a common behavioural pattern in the narcissist.

Jay is drawn to Lara because he recognises her need to care for others, so knows she'll provide what he's looking for.

Jay: *"I spotted immediately that Lara's the type of girl who likes to take care of people and it's nice to have someone making sure the small stuff is dealt with."*

What Jay's doesn't see is the deeper psychological draw governing both his and Lara's attraction: their mutually shared problem of feelings of personal inadequacy.

On the surface Jay believes himself special and different,

but it's important to note that narcissism can often mask deep-seated feelings of insecurity and worthlessness, hidden from the conscious mind through the creation of a false self.

These disavowed feelings generate a desire to belittle others and a strong tendency towards moodiness and depression if the narcissist believes they've fallen short of 'perfection'.

Jay is superficially attracted to Lara because she's prepared to place his needs before her own, but on a deeper level something more insidious is happening: Jay is unconsciously passing his own feelings of worthlessness onto Lara.

Lara is experiencing projective identification.

---

## DEFINITION

Projective identification is a complex psychological state, but at its heart it's essentially a game of 'emotional pass the parcel', where undesired and difficult feelings are passed from one person to the other without either being aware of what's happening. Often in intimate relationships, but also in more casual encounters, we find ourselves experiencing feelings that belong as much to the other person as to ourselves. When this occurs, we are experiencing projective identification.

---

In choosing Lara, Jay is unconsciously protecting himself from feelings of personal inadequacy through unconsciously forcing them into her.

Why doesn't Lara question her sense of growing inadequacy?

Because Lara's already lacking in self-worth she's primed to pick up Jay's unconscious feelings of worthlessness. She therefore doesn't question why her own feelings are becoming more intense.

Lara: *"In many ways I've never felt that good about myself."*

Ultimately, however, Jay's not responsible for Lara's behaviour; she is. So, whilst it's clear he's exploiting her, it's important to look more closely at what's happening, to identify what Lara's also gaining from the relationship.

A useful method for doing this is the drama triangle.

# THE DRAMA TRIANGLE

First conceptualised by Stephen Karpman, a pupil of Eric Berne, the drama triangle delineates the roles we often unconsciously adopt when caught in conflict or power play. It can be a useful tool in analysing interpersonal relationships.

Each point on the triangle denotes a specific role:

1.  victim
2.  persecutor
3.  rescuer.

If three people are playing it's generally easy to identify which point they've placed themselves on, but two people can still successfully engage, simply by switching from one point to the other in quick succession.

Most of us have a preferred role (e.g. the person who loves to rescue) but it's important to note we all switch places, so that even during a comparatively short interaction our roles can shift unpredictably.

To further complicate matters, two roles can appear to be played out simultaneously: how many people do you know who persecute from the position of the 'victim'?

We must therefore look beneath the surface of any interaction if we really want to know what's happening.

So, where are Lara and Jay on the triangle?

Lara is caught in the roles of both 'victim' and 'rescuer', switching periodically between the two.

She wishes to make everything easy for Jay, rescuing him from financial incompetence and freeing him from domestic drudgery. Yet all she apparently receives in return is persecution. Jay constantly subjects her to angry mood swings and extreme selfishness, until she feels exhausted and victimised.

How then can Jay feel victimised by Lara?

In a subtle way Lara's much closer to the role of 'persecutor' than she realises. She's becoming increasingly frustrated by Jay's behaviour, but her lack of self-worth and fear of abandonment are preventing her from openly expressing this frustration, or even consciously acknowledging its existence.

At present Lara's frustration is being expressed through tears, an emotional response allied to the position of 'victim'. But frustration also contains anger and, as Lara is unable to express a feeling so ill-suited to the role of 'victim' or 'rescuer', Jay is unconsciously expressing it on her behalf.

And here we return to projective identification.

Lara is unconsciously forcing Jay to act out her rage. If Jay is the angry one, Lara can continue in the position of 'victim', thereby occupying the moral high ground.

Just as Jay has found the perfect candidate to pick up his feelings of worthlessness, so too Lara has chosen well in Jay. Each unconsciously acts out a disavowed aspect of the other's personality, but because that aspect is strikingly familiar, neither suspects what is happening.

By unconsciously compounding their own already-entrenched emotional positions, Lara and Jay are becoming further removed from a more complete understanding of who they truly are.

It's a curious phenomenon both in couples and groups that, because unexpressed emotions seek an outlet, if a person is either unwilling or unable to express how they're feeling, then someone else will unconsciously act it out on their behalf. We can often become unwitting participants in a confused cocktail of emotions where no one understands what's going on.

Jay is half aware of Lara's anger, however, even if she's not conscious of it herself, and this is one of the reasons why he feels controlled and essentially persecuted by her. His assumption that Lara is enabling his dependency to meet her own co-dependent need is also correct. Yet, to an outsider, Jay is the sole 'persecutor'.

As with Lara, Jay completely fails to recognise his own complicity.

His anger at Lara's control is as much an expression of Jay's own unconscious feelings of inadequacy as it is a reaction to her inability to openly express rage. Instead of assuming responsibility and actively taking control of his life, Jay accuses Lara of trapping him.

Because of the shifting nature of the drama triangle, Jay himself temporarily adopts the position of the 'rescuer' when Lara bursts into tears. But, as Lara's grief is mixed with rage, he's quickly catapulted back into the position of 'persecutor', unconsciously forced into expressing Lara's disavowed emotion.

Neither Jay nor Lara is conscious of what's happening, so their relationship continues to spiral downwards.

# POSITIVE STEPS FOR CHANGE

## LARA

Lara needs to actively acknowledge at least some of the frustration and anger she's feeling, if she is to have any chance of escaping this vicious cycle.

To an outsider like Ginny there's incomprehension at her continued complicity in Jay's behaviour, and this reflects the confusion onlookers often feel when witnessing the co-dependent's willingness to remain in a dysfunctional relationship.

Presently Lara's so wedded to the position of 'victim' that she's unable to recognise her self-subjugation is destructive both to herself and Jay. Letting go of the need to be the caring one who's never angry or openly judgemental will be extremely difficult, as it strikes at the heart of how she's come to define herself.

Because anger can often be used to bully and threaten others, our view of it is largely negative. In situations of chronic disempowerment, however, it can reconnect us to our own life force and positively demonstrate our capacity for agency.

This isn't to underestimate Lara's underlying grief. Her feelings of worthlessness and fear of abandonment need to be thoroughly explored.

If she can access some of the frustration and anger she's experiencing, it will give her the strength to make changes.

One way to achieve this is for Lara to consciously reframe her role in relation to Jay: if Lara can recognise she's enabling Jay's dependency out of an unconscious need to control, then her role as the caring one will start to look more complex and less attractive.

Lara is fleeing her *Shadow*. Ultimately this is impossible. The disowned parts of the self will always find us, even if they must be acted out by someone else.

It's ironic that in times of crises or self-doubt those very aspects we have unconsciously sought to deny are often what we most need. Recognition and acknowledgement of these disavowed parts can reconnect us to our essential selves and help us become more powerful and fully rounded human beings.

No one can escape issues of power and personal autonomy when it comes to personal relationships.

# JAY

Jay's in an unenviable position. He's going to find it extremely difficult to relinquish his overarching sense of personal importance, because this will require acknowledging feelings of inadequacy and self-doubt.

The fact Jay wants to leave, however, suggests he's trapped by laziness and self-entitlement far more than by a need to persecute Lara. It's Lara, rather than Jay, who's unconsciously driving the dynamic of 'victim' and 'persecutor'.

Jay has more to gain from greater self-awareness than he realises. If he can access some of his own self-doubt, he will gain emotionally in ways he's not expecting.

Grandiosity is an isolating experience. If we can't acknowledge feelings of inadequacy and shame, even in our closest relationships, neither can we experience true intimacy.

## TOGETHER

If Lara and Jay are going to stand any chance of staying together they are going to need help. It's unlikely that such deeply entrenched patterns can be resolved without some form of external assistance and they will need couples' counselling.

Although Lara isn't living with someone at the extreme end of addiction, she could also attend CoDa, an organisation of self-help groups actively seeking to create healthier relationships.

It's unlikely, however, that either Lara or Jay will develop a sufficient level of emotional understanding swiftly enough to save their relationship. Lara is much better off without Jay.

'The Art of Giving', as with all the Games in this book, is essentially about looking beneath the surface of our thoughts and actions. This can be particularly difficult when we're trapped in a co-dependent pattern, as even superficial possession of the moral high ground is very hard to relinquish. Yet, unless there's a willingness to scrutinise both our actions and feelings, we will not escape the cycle.

# EPILOGUE

## LARA

"Jay's gone. He left last Saturday after the most dreadful scene and I don't know what to do with myself... it's awful.

He'd been in a terrible mood all day and basically barricaded himself into Claire's old room, insisting he needed some privacy.

I'd stayed in... worried he'd end up angry if I left... but by eight o'clock, when he still hadn't emerged, I was starting to feel quite concerned.

After another twenty minutes I quietly tapped on the door... just to ask if he wanted a cup of tea, and he flew out of the room in an absolute rage!

God, it was terrifying, he'd never shouted like that before. Then, right in the middle of his awful tirade, the police showed up!

I found out later the neighbours had called them, but at the time I didn't know what was going on. I thought they were going to arrest Jay, so I started pleading... trying to explain what was happening... saying that everything was ok. But it wasn't. When they finally left he packed his bags and headed out of the door at once... and now I feel completely alone.

*Carla came round on Sunday, to take me out for breakfast. I'd called her sobbing at 2 o'clock in the morning. She kept on saying what an arrogant sh\*t he was and how much better off I was without him, but that's not how it feels.*

*Everyone always leaves me... even Jay. What an earth am I doing wrong? I couldn't give more if I tried! I'm completely exhausted by it all.*

*'You give too much,' said Ginny, when I saw her a couple of days later.*

*I'm really starting to hate that girl! What does she know about it?*

*He's not coming back though, that's for sure."*

# JAY

*"Thank God I'm out of there! What a nightmare!*

*It came to a head last Saturday evening in the worst way possible... and all because of Lara and her sh\*tty cup of tea!*

*I'd had a terrible week, frustrating and difficult, with no work done and a vile letter from the bank, kindly informing me of how bad my finances are. As if I didn't know.*

*I'd shut myself in my study... desperate to focus... but absolutely nothing came. Until finally... after Christ knows how many hours, I actually got in the flow.*

*Then it happened... of course it did... Lara tapped on the door! For f\*ck's sake! I couldn't help myself; I just went completely ballistic!*

*The next thing I knew, the police were hammering on the door whilst Lara sat wailing in a corner.*

*I thought I was going to be arrested! I would have been if she hadn't pleaded for me. But do you know what? Part of me would have preferred it if they had just taken me away, I felt so completely at her mercy!*

*I packed immediately; I just had to get out of there... It was mad!*

*So, I'm back at Nick's... on the petty proviso I pull my weight with the washing up. I don't care. Anything's better than that!*

*Nick's friend Mat said he might have some freelance work, to help get me out of this hole... and needless to say Liddy's been completely unsympathetic. Apparently, I've treated Lara 'appallingly'. Christ, that pisses me off! If Liddy had been on the inside of that relationship she wouldn't be so cocksure.*

*It's not the first time I've been told I'm selfish, and perhaps I can be, but there was something about that situation that really drove me crazy. If Lara wasn't happy about things, why didn't she say?!*

*I get so sick of always being the one who's blamed! Is that who I am?"*

# HOUSE OF CARDS

## THE TALE OF TOM AND GWEN

# TOM'S TALE

"I bumped into an old friend last Thursday, quite out of the blue, in the Nag's Head pub near King Street. A group of us had knocked off early from work and were out for a bit of a laugh when I spotted him.

'Christ!' I thought. 'Ben Bradshaw! It's been ages.'

He was propping up the bar at the end of the room deep in a pie and a pint, but he must have felt me watching him because he looked up and caught my eye. We smiled, and I sidled over.

'Hey, mate, how are you?'

Ben and I used to work together. He's got a wicked sense of humour and an eye for the girls and we'd often have a drink and a joke down the pub before we headed home. A few times he even came back to mine and Gwen would cook us supper; she's pretty good like that. But then he changed companies and life moved on and I guess we just lost touch.

After the usual banter he asked how Gwen was. 'Fine,' I said. I didn't want to get into it... not with Ben. It would've sounded like whinging and who wants to listen to that.

'You're lucky there, mate,' Ben retorted. 'Knock-out figure and a first-rate cook. I'd hang on to her if I were you.'

Am I lucky? I certainly used to think so. So, what's going wrong?

*Gwen is the girl I'd always dreamed of. The first thing I noticed... after I'd clocked her looks... was just how easy-going she seemed. She loves her job and has plenty of friends, so it's never felt like a drag. We moved in together after just six months and the following year was fantastic. But lately things haven't felt quite the same. It's nothing worth fighting over... just a mountain of niggles, but, God, it's annoying.*

*You want an example? Well, one thing that's getting on my nerves right now is this ongoing thing with my mum. We always used to see her for tea together, every other Sunday in the month. Gwen was happy to come along... at least I thought she was, but the past few times there's always been a reason why she can't seem to make it. She's so apologetic I don't feel able to complain and to be honest I didn't even realise it was bothering me... that is, until the other day. Gwen asked if I was coming to her sister's birthday and I told her I'd booked something in. It wasn't true... well, not until later... but her sister really gets on my nerves, so why should I bother when she doesn't?*

*Another thing – and I know it's small – Gwen's stopped making me cups of tea; she used to, all the time. So, I've stopped bringing her tea in the morning... why should I?*

*If there's a programme she feels like watching, she just does. I could have had a crap day and really need to talk but no, she's sorry, she must see this right now.*

*It's been building slowly for the past few months, but then last Saturday things really turned sour... in the supermarket of all places.*

*I don't usually go... why should I? Gwen does pretty much all the cooking. But I wanted to make the effort that day and thought it would be appreciated. Apparently not.*

*Gwen's on some sort of health food kick and I've been going along with it, even though I'm not that bothered. You can definitely have too much of a good thing, however, so when we found ourselves passing the jams I reached over and pulled down a jar of Nutella. That's it... just that. The next thing I know she's giving me this look... like I've committed some sort of crime!*

*'Really!' she said, and her eyebrow went up in this totally withering way. I'm not joking, I couldn't believe it! I felt so humiliated.*

*'For Christ's sake!' I responded. 'One jar of Nutella!... Don't touch the chocolate spread, folks!'*

*Some guy across the aisle grinned and Gwen's face screwed up. I thought we might actually get into a fight... something that never happens with her. But, no... she just looked like a pinched grapefruit, then started to back down.*

*'I know, I know. I'm sorry. It's just we're supposed to be cutting down, that's all... but it's nothing. Let's get to the checkout, yeah.'*

*'You're right, it's nothing!' I was so annoyed!*

*'I'm sorry, ok.'*

*We made it home and Gwen went out. Apparently, she'd already arranged to see Liz... though she certainly hadn't mentioned it earlier. When she got back it was late and I couldn't be bothered to get into an argument. So I said nothing, and she said nothing either. Then the following morning she made a great breakfast and I decided to let it go. Life's too short.*

*Nevertheless, the whole situation's really starting to get on my nerves and I've found myself wondering if our relationship's worth the hassle.*

*I never thought I'd feel this way about Gwen and part of me knows Ben's right, Gwen's great; but freedom is looking pretty tempting right now. Having a girlfriend shouldn't be hard work, right?*

*It feels like we're heading towards a serious fall and I know I need to say something, I'm just not sure how. She hasn't really done anything and I could be opening a can of worms. You never know, it might just blow over if I wait it out."*

# GWEN'S TALE

*"So, what can I say about Tom? That's tough. I really don't feel like talking about it. Still, here goes.*

*Tom can be great in so many ways, but the one thing that stands out right now... is how he expects his own way about everything.*

*We met a few years ago at a picnic in the park and I fell for him almost immediately. It was one of those random events posted on Facebook, where miraculously the sun kept shining and everyone had a great time.*

*Tom was the life and soul of the party... he can really put people at their ease... and with his super-toned body and great sense of humour it wasn't long before I wanted his attention. So, when he flopped down casually on the rug next to mine I offered him a large slice of apple pie and smiled.*

*'Did you bake this?'*

*'Yep.'*

*'Wow! It's delicious. I don't think we've met. I'm Tom.'*

*'Hi Tom. I'm Gwen... it's a pleasure.'*

*Things just seemed to go from there and the first six months were amazing. When he suggested we move in together I didn't think twice. Finally, someone who was not only fun but who amazingly I fancied as well! My kind of guy.*

*But living together has really started to get on my nerves.*

*I pride myself on being easy-going. Everyone comments on it... they always have... and I know it was a big plus for Tom. Some people, however, really know how to take the piss and it turns out Tom is one of them.*

*He often comes home late from work, after one too many down the pub. Annoying enough in itself, you'd think, but then he'll randomly bring back a friend... with the first I know about it their drunken laughter on the doorstep. In the early days I was eager to please, so I'd slap on a smile, cook them some food, then wash up the dishes afterwards. Tom would say thank you, which sort of made it ok, I guess, but he rarely even bothers to do that anymore. So now, if I cook for him plus his mates, I find myself starting to fume.*

*Nine times out of ten the weekend works according to Tom: seeing his mum, meeting his friends... everything just to suit him. Don't get me wrong, he likes to have a bit of 'together time', but it's always fitted round football and the all-important after-match drink. As long I tow the line... his perfect girlfriend... everything stays just fine.*

*Increasingly however, I'm fighting back. Not openly, of course... how can I? I'm supposed to be easy-going Gwen... and, anyway, who wants an argument? There's nothing worse. But in little ways I'm starting to stand my ground, and I think he's finally noticing.*

*I don't run around making him cups of tea anymore and I certainly don't drop everything just to listen to Tom's problems. If I'm not in the mood to visit his mum, I don't... in fact, the weekends are about me now.*

*He's changing too, but not in a good way. It isn't just the lack of thanks for all those meals; it's a thousand little things... too many to mention... although a couple do spring to mind. Tom doesn't even bother making me tea in the morning, and I'm sure he deliberately found something to do on my sister's birthday. Compared to how I run around him it makes very little difference, but you'd think he would have upped his game in response to my actions... not got even worse!*

*Then last Saturday things really deteriorated.*

*I generally do a big shop at Sainsbury's, so the week days are easier to manage. But you can be sure Tom won't bother to come. As far as he's concerned I'm in charge of the weekly groceries and, since I'm responsible for nearly all the cooking, I guess it makes sense.*

*But this time he offered to join me. 'Wow!' I thought. 'Maybe he's trying to make an effort, perhaps he's starting to appreciate everything I do.' Not so.*

*Tom's been putting on weight just recently. He's commented on it himself and we've both agreed to cut down on the sugary stuff for a while... no biscuits or chocolate, that sort of thing. Anyway... we were going down the aisles and making good progress, but then as we came to the jams and spreads he reached right past me and grabbed a jar of Nutella.*

*I know it sounds petty, but in that moment I realised: Tom wasn't being thoughtful at all; he just wanted to ensure his share of the sweets!*

*I must have flashed him a look and I'm guessing I made a brief comment... because he turned on me suddenly in such a vile way and said something jokily snide! Some guy cocked his head, then smirked, and I felt completely humiliated. I backed down immediately... what else could I do... but when we got home I just packed away the things and left. I told him I'd already made plans to see Liz. It wasn't true... I just had to get out and talk things through.*

*Liz was lovely, but she just kept saying that if I didn't tell him how I was feeling it could all start to go seriously wrong. Easy to say, but definitely not so easy to do.*

*I hate any form of confrontation. People never seem to react well and, judging by the incident in the supermarket, neither will Tom. The last thing I want is to be accused of being a nag and I don't see why I should have to spell out the fact that my feelings ought to be taken into consideration. It should be perfectly obvious to anyone.*

*When I got home we barely spoke and I spent the whole night worrying about what would happen next. So, at nine in the morning I got out of bed and cooked him a full English breakfast. After that the mood noticeably softened.*

*I don't want to lose Tom. I still really love him. He's warm and funny and a lot of the time we get along fine. But I can feel the resentment building and whilst people say arguments clear the air sometimes they just make things worse. I don't know what to do."*

# WHAT'S THE GAME?

Like all the Games we've examined so far, 'House of Cards' can be analysed from several different angles. What it most clearly illustrates, however, is the progressively negative impact of passive aggression.

> ## DEFINITION
>
> Passive aggression is an indirect expression of hostility. Whenever a person repeatedly forgets, delays or prevaricates, flashes a 'look', finds an excuse, or just sulks, they're being passive aggressive.

Passive aggression is the guerrilla warfare of human relationships. It is utilised in both the personal and professional spheres whenever there is either an unwillingness or inability to exert direct strength.

Like any method of slow-drip subterfuge, passive aggression should not be underestimated in its capacity to frustrate and control. If both parties choose to adopt this tactic it can steadily errode a relationship as successfully as open conflict.

189

# TOM AND GWEN

By repeatedly expressing their feelings of frustration through evasive and unspoken means, Tom and Gwen are in danger of irreparably damaging their relationship.

# TOM

Tom is used to getting his own way and part of his attraction to Gwen is her willingness to go along with this.

Tom: *"The first thing I noticed... after I'd clocked her looks... was just how easy-going she seemed."*

Unlike Jay in 'The Art of Giving', Tom's attitude stands clearly within the bounds of normal behaviour and as such is less likely to be commented on by others. If Gwen's not willing to bring it to his attention, why would he change?

Presently Tom isn't even aware he's being selfish, although

he's certainly noticed Gwen's altered her behaviour. But instead of asking what's wrong he's simply reacting in kind.

It's not until the incident in the supermarket that any form of open confrontation occurs. The inappropriate circumstances and apparently trivial nature of the argument, however, undermines the possibility of an honest exchange.

Tom and Gwen have displaced their mutual frustration onto a jar of Nutella.

# DISPLACEMENT

### DEFINITION

Displacement is one of the more common devices found in our emotional toolbox. It occurs when we unconsciously shift our feelings of anger at one situation onto an unrelated and often banal incident, which we then respond to with disproportionate rage.

For Tom and Gwen, it's the drip-drip effect of many frustrations that results in the supermarket outburst; in other scenarios it could be anger related to a single significant but unresolved event, unintentionally triggered by someone's actions or comments.

Why doesn't Tom just ask Gwen what's wrong?

Up until now Tom's been satisfied with the status quo. If he openly questions Gwen and she honestly responds, he will be forced to address what's happening and things might change.

There's also the danger Tom could ask what's wrong, but Gwen replies evasively. How many times have you heard or given the answer 'I'm fine', when the opposite is true? You may be aware you're frustrating the enquirer and making things worse, but you do it anyway.

Both people must be willing to risk an honest conversation for any shift to occur, but the attitude is often taken that if nothing's openly said things "*might just blow over*".

Judging by their present trajectory, however, if Tom and Gwen avoid confronting their problems the relationship will further deteriorate until Tom leaves. Tom will then cite Gwen's change in attitude as his reason for ending it.

This brings us to the other appeal of passive aggression:

Passive aggression has the seductive potential of being a convenient tool to evade blame. We *know* we're angry and are generally aware of how frustrating our behaviour is, but by remaining careful not to openly express our feelings it's the other person who often appears the unreasonable or angry one.

Tom and Gwen are both self-righteously nursing their private grievances, but neither is willing to assume responsibility for saying how they feel.

If Tom and Gwen were to communicate openly, not only would both be forced to hear the other's point of view but the behaviour of each, with all its anger and confusion, would be placed in the spotlight. In saying nothing, neither of them runs that risk.

If Tom walks out without an honest conversation he won't understand what went wrong and everything will remain Gwen's fault.

In many ways Tom's expectations of Gwen suggests he unconsciously sees her as 'mum'. This is helping to foster the belief that his needs should come first, and up until now Gwen has gone along with it.

Because Tom and Gwen are already living together, if pushed they'll probably be honest about how they're feeling. The problem is it may come too late.

'House of Cards' is an apt metaphor for this Game. If too many grievances start to build, eventually the structure will collapse. It's always better to address a situation sooner rather than later.

At present Tom's conflicted about what to do, but it's important to note that in doing nothing he's still making a choice; things will further deteriorate.

# GWEN

Gwen's passive aggression has a different hue. She's angry at Tom's behaviour but worried if she directly confronts him the relationship will fall apart.

Gwen: *"When I got home we barely spoke and I spent the whole night worrying about what would happen next."'*

Nothing is openly said about Gwen's past, so we have little understanding of why she's reluctant to express her feelings, but one thing's clear: Gwen has learnt that life's easier if she's accommodating.

In 'Through the Looking Glass' we observed how families, both consciously and unconsciously, push us towards a pattern of behaviour that fits the family structure. Gwen appears to have been 'easy-going Gwen' and this has become her dominant role in adult life.

There's a hint towards the end of her narrative that one of Gwen's parents may have been pigeonholed as a *"nag"*. She's certainly wary of being pushed in that direction.

Gwen: *"The last thing I want is to be accused of being a nag and I don't see why I should have to spell out the fact that my feelings ought to be taken into consideration."*

The role of 'nag' is a useful example of someone unconsciously forced to act out a negative pattern of behaviour for the benefit of others. Often, frustration at an unfair distribution of domestic chores spills out into petty complaints, and when this happens the laid-back attitude of everyone else is essentially achieved at the 'nag's' expense.

Because Gwen's unused to expressing difficult emotions, her anger is being displaced onto trivia. This is leaving Gwen at risk of appearing the very person she dreads: the woman who nags over a jar of Nutella.

Gwen: *"I hate any form of confrontation. People never seem to react well, and judging by the incident in the supermarket, neither will Tom."*

In attempting to shift our style of relating, however, we're always battling with at least three difficulties:

1.  Our newly formed actions are bound to be clunky. We're likely to react in an inappropriate and heavy-handed manner, and this will create a desire to scurry back to our former patterns of behaviour.

2.  Those closest to us will nearly always have either a conscious or unconscious investment in maintaining the status quo, so we're unlikely to receive much support. (Even if we're behaving badly and everyone consciously

longs for change, their unconscious motivations won't always match their conscious desires. Dysfunctional families will often create a *scapegoat*. This is the person unconsciously assigned to act out a family's dysfunction. If that scapegoat chooses to 'resign', then the other family members will be forced to confront their own dysfunction.)

3. We ourselves have a strong emotional investment in maintaining the status quo. We know what to say and how others will respond. We may not like it but it's familiar to us.

Gwen's friend Liz, whilst offering sound advice, only has a partial understanding of what Gwen's up against. Liz will be aware Gwen's worried the relationship might end, but she may not realise how hard it is for Gwen to change.

Judging, however, by the level of anger and frustration Gwen's feeling, she needs to make the shift. Even if her relationship breaks down Gwen could use this experience to clarify what she wants in the future.

# POSITIVE STEPS FOR CHANGE

So where do Gwen and Tom go from here?

Gwen and Tom like each other. If they can be honest about their feelings, there's a very real chance the relationship could work. But they need to find a way of exploring what's happening in a way that feels safe for Gwen.

A useful tool to employ for this is Transactional Analysis. TA offers a clear and sensible framework for a difficult conversation and can help take the heat out of strong emotion.

We focused on TA in 'Noughts and Crosses' and I refer you back to that chapter for a detailed analysis of a 'transaction'.

For expediency, however, I will run through the theory again.

Whilst broad in scope and multi-faceted in structure, at its most basic, Transactional Analysis is just that: the step-by-step analysis of a conversation, verbal or non-verbal, occurring between two or more people.

TA posits the theory that our minds are divided into three separate ego states, *Parent Adult* and *Child*, and in any interaction we are consciously or unconsciously relating to each other from one of these three 'states'.

The terms Parent, Adult, Child do not have the same meaning as they do in everyday language; they are more complex, fluid and nuanced than any literal meaning would imply. There are, however, similarities:

* The *Parent* is the deep-rooted voice of authority, planted by figures of our childhood.
* The *Adult* is that aspect of ourselves able to consider and evaluate what is happening in the present.
* The *Child* represents our feeling selves, often dominant when we are experiencing strong emotion.

If two people wish to embark on a highly charged conversation, staying in the Adult position enables each to hear what the other is trying to say.

By approaching a difficult exchange from the place of the Adult, an attitude of non-confrontation is fostered, and with it the desire to approach a problem in a spirit of openness and compromise.

In the absence of a mediator, consciously adopting TA's framework is invaluable; the key is always a willingness for mutual honesty.

At the very least, it's important to preface any conversation with a clear statement that you wish to work out what's going on, rather than simply accuse. The need of the other party to defend their position is immediately lessened, and the stark polarisation that often accompanies an airing of views can be headed off at the pass.

# TOM

Although we haven't looked at the potential origins of Tom's behaviour, he will be caught in his own patterns as much as Gwen, and these will be governing his expectations of her.

If Tom can recognise his unconscious positioning of Gwen as 'mum', then hopefully he won't feel he's making quite such an effort simply by accompanying her to the supermarket.

People can often slide into the parent/child dynamic in a way which runs far deeper than the Parent/Child transactions tracked by TA. If this is acceptable to both parties it's entirely up to them; the problem occurs when it's having a negative impact on their relationship.

Deep-seated patterns can be very hard to shift, and TA offers a useful starting point to discuss what's happening.

# GWEN

Although Gwen is increasingly resentful of the position she finds herself in, she has never learnt how to openly explore a relationship problem. This is contributing to her fear of doing so. Tom, ironically, is less likely to leave if Gwen addresses their difficulties directly, but emotional insecurity is contributing to her silence.

The supermarket episode was felt by Gwen to be humiliating, but it must be noted that whilst Tom reacted by trying to undermine her, this was largely because he felt humiliated himself. Had Gwen been more confident, she could have let his reaction lie there, then invited a frank conversation on their return home. Instead she attempted to mollify his rage.

Gwen may have been used to seeing someone in her childhood, systematically undermined by others, so is responding with a learnt pattern of behaviour. She needs to become more aware of this, if she is to have any hope of shifting the pattern. Whilst change is unlikely to be radical, even after the issues are addressed, it can be incremental and with practice things will improve.

# EPILOGUE

## GWEN

*"We stayed at my parents' last weekend. It's a bit of a trek but I wanted to make the effort. Saturday afternoon was sunny, and Dad was larking about in the garden with my niece Becky. Tom had gone to a football match with Jonathan, and Katy was reading a magazine. Mum was standing at the kitchen sink making Dad a cup of tea... nothing unusual in that.*

*Mum looked tired, she often does, and I watched as she absent-mindedly spooned two sugars into the cup... Dad hates sugar. Then as she started to stir the tea... carefully now... I knew exactly why she'd done it. I love my dad, he's such great fun, but, God, it's wearisome always being the one who everyone takes for granted. No wonder Mum gets her own back sometimes, let alone nags occasionally. And, as for our jokes at her expense, I feel quite ashamed to think of them now... particularly when I remember the scene in the supermarket.*

*Tom and my brother bounced through the door, laughing and full of the game. I immediately retreated to the living room... I just wasn't in the mood for their behaviour.*

*Then it occurred to me, what was I worried about? Did I*

*honestly think Tom would leave just because I asked him to pull his weight?*

*Mum's never had any confidence. She's constantly worrying what Dad might say and I sometimes wonder if she's scared he'll leave her. But has he ever left? No. Why would he? He's lucky to have her! And if Tom left? So what? Better than spending the rest of my life being taken for granted, that's for sure.*

*I thought it through carefully that evening... determined not to launch into some sort of rant. Then the following morning on the drive back home I told him exactly what was on my mind.*

*'Look,' I said, 'I definitely don't want to turn into a nag, but it would really be helpful if you could make more of an effort over the little things... helping with the housework, texting when you're going to be late or are bringing a friend back home... that sort of thing. I know it sounds trivial, but it would make my life so much easier and create an enormous difference in our relationship.'*

*Tom seemed genuinely surprised and claimed he had no idea how much things were bothering me!*

*'Why didn't you say? I'm not a mind reader, Gwen! I had no idea what was bothering you... and, as for the house stuff, I thought you wanted to be in charge?'*

*'Fair point, perhaps I do... sometimes, but cleaning up other people's crap can get pretty wearisome, you know.'*

*I'm not imagining Tom's going to change overnight – in fact, I'm sure he won't – but I'm not prepared to put up with it any longer and I'm going to make a real effort to keep the lines of communication open. And if he walks? Well, you can be certain I'll be clearer about my own needs next time."*

# TOM

*"Gwen finally spoke her mind, thank God! I think both of us had really had enough.*

*It was on the way back from her parent's house, before we'd stopped off at the pub. I'd had no idea she felt so annoyed... though I was certainly starting to guess. If I'm honest I should have spoken up too... nothing is solved by stewing. It seems ridiculous now to imagine it would be.*

*Gwen's comments reminded me of Mum in a way... she can be pretty stern if things get out of hand. At least Gwen wants to hear my point of view, which Mum rarely does.*

*To be honest, I feel quite relieved, even though it's obvious that I'm going to have pull my weight a bit more. It's as if a line's been drawn and we both know where we stand.*

*I know, I know, I should have done more in the first place, but it's not always easy, you know. It's a lot simpler if someone just speaks up.*

*Gwen's a great girl and I do want to make it work with her. If we can both be a bit more honest about how we're feeling, maybe we'll get there and really commit for the long haul."*

# CONCLUSION

Not all our relationship patterns are dysfunctional. Many are positive and some are simply neutral.

In the concluding narrative of 'House of Cards' Tom's positive response to Gwen's direct expression of frustration can in part be attributed to how it reminds him of his own mother's behaviour.

Tom: *"Gwen's comments reminded me of Mum in a way... she can be pretty stern if things get out of hand. At least Gwen wants to hear my point of view, which Mum rarely does."*

Gwen's directness is familiar to Tom, so he immediately feels at ease.

Tom: *"A line's been drawn and we both know where we stand."*

What Tom's comparison clearly illustrates, is that even when Gwen speaks from an Adult position the past isn't fully escaped. We often like or dislike people simply because their behavioural patterns remind us of a significant past relationship. Yet, even when our reaction is positive, every time we respond in this way it serves to obscure our understanding of the person who's actually present.

Increased self-awareness can help us notice when we're transferring our feelings for one individual unthinkingly onto another, rather than seeing the new person for who they really are.

This book focuses on the patterns that inhibit our ability to relate positively to others. These patterns should not be underestimated; an unconscious compulsion to repeat what we know whilst it can be made conscious can never be fully unlearnt.

In some cases, our patterns are so ingrained that awareness alone isn't enough to shift them single-handedly. This is when professional assistance in the form of an experienced psychotherapist or self-help group could be the most appropriate course of action. The co-dependency organisation CoDa, mentioned in 'The Art of Giving', is a group open to all.

Emotional shifts are always possible once we're committed to change.

We're all capable of loving and worthy of being loved. If your childhood experiences have taught you otherwise, please let this book speak to you.